LEVINSON
267-9151

לוי

מ"ל

TEFILLIN

An Illustrated Guide to their Makeup and Use

by

Mosheh Chanina Neiman

Translated and prepared for publication by

Dovid Oratz

FELDHEIM
Jerusalem □ New York

Jerusalem, 5755

This work appeared originally in Hebrew
as the two-volume set,
Hanachas Tefillin k'Hilchasah
and
Hakaras ha-Tefillin v'Chelkeihen
which received the approbations of
Halachic authorities in Eretz Yisrael.

Technical Layouts: Shmuel Balsam, Architect
Illustrations: Yonatan Gerstein

First published 1995
ISBN 0-87306-711-8
Copyright © 1995 by
Mosheh Chanina Neiman
Besht 13, Bnei Brak, Israel

FELDHEIM PUBLISHERS
200 Airport Executive Park
Nanuet, NY 10954

POB 35002 / Jerusalem, Israel

Printed in Israel

Rabbi CHAIM P. SCHEINBERG

Rosh Hayeshiva "TORAH-ORE"

and Morah Hora'ah of Kiryat Mattersdorf

הרב חיים פינחס שיינברג

ראש ישיבת "תורה-אור"

ומורה הוראה דקרית מטרסדורף

ב"ה ערב שבת תשנ"ג

הנני מכיר את הרב ר' דוד שליט"א יותר מעשרים שנה
וכעת הביא לי תרגום של הספר התפילין - הכרת התפילין
וחלקיהם בתוספת מדריק להנחת תפילין מהספר הנחת תפילין
כהלכתה. והנה שבחו הספרים הנ"ל בעברית קולי של הרק
והיות שיש צורך לספר כזה לדוברי אנגלית גם הנני מברך
את המחברם שליצית בכל דרכו וחזקה על אבר שאינו
מוציא ידו דבר שאינו מתוקן!

לכבוד שמע הברכה ולהעביר

חיים פינחס שיינ(ברג)

בס"ד

ט"ז טבת תשנ"ד

הנני מכיר את הרב דוד ארץ שליט"א יותר מעשרים שנה, וכעת הביא לי תרגום של הספר
"התפילין - הכרת התפילין וחלקיהן" בתוספת מדריך להנחת תפילין מהספר "הנחת
תפילין כהלכתה". והנה שבחו את הספרים הנ"ל בעברית גדולי בני ברק. והיות שיש צורך
לספר כזה לדוברי אנגלית, גם כן הנני מברך את הרב דוד ארץ שליט"א שיצליח בכל דרכיו,
וחזקה על חבר שאינו מוציא מתחת ידו דבר שאינו מתוקן!

רחוב פנים מאירות 2, ירושלים, ת. ד. 6979, טל. 371513-(02), ישראל
2, Panim Meirot St., Jerusalem, P. O. B. 6979, Tel (02)-371513, Israel

RABBI TOVIA GOLDSTEIN
1718 - 59TH STREET
BROOKLYN, N. Y. 11204
256-2018

טובי' גאלדשטיין
ראש הישיבה
ישיבת עמק הלכה
ברוקלין, נ. י.

בס"ד

הנה כבוד תלמידי הרב ר' דוד חיים ארץ שליט"א אשר למד כמה
שנים בישיבתנו הק' והצליח מאוד בתורה וביראת שמים, וחוץ מזה
הוא בעל מידות תרומיות, וכעת תרגם ללשון אנגלי' את הספר
הכרת התפילין וחלקיהן, בצירוף מדריך להנחת תפילין [ועל גוף
הספר כבר שבחוהו גדולי ישראל שליט"א] וחברי הכולל עיינו
בהמתורגם ואמרו שתרגם הכל בדיוק גדול, וחזקה על חבר שאינו
מוציא מתחת ידו דבר שאינו מתוקן.

ואני מברך אותו שיצליח בלימודו ויזכה ללמוד
מתוך הרחבת הדעת.

ידידו המברכו בכל לב
טובי' גאלדשטיין

היום יום א' כ"ח כסליו ד' דחנוכה, שנת תשנ"ד
פה ברוקלין

בס"ד

הנה כבוד תלמידי הרב ר' דוד חיים ארץ שליט"א אשר למד כמה שנים בישיבתנו הק' והצליח מאוד בתורה וביראת שמים, וחוץ מזה הוא בעל מידות תרומיות, וכעת תרגם בלשון "אנגלי" את הספר הכרת התפילין וחלקיהן בצירוף מדריך להנחת תפילין [ועל גוף הספר כבר שבחוהו גדולי ישראל בארץ ישראל שליט"א], וחברי הכולל עיינו בהמתורגם ואמרו שתרגם הכל בדיוק גדול, וחזקה על חבר שאינו מוציא מתחת ידו דבר שאינו מתוקן.

ואני מברך אותו שיצליח בלימודו ויזכה ללמוד מתוך הרחבת הדעת.

ידידו המברכו בכל לב

Table of Contents

Introduction

The Mitzvah of Wearing Tefillin

The tefillin represent some of the most important concepts in Judaism. These concepts will be analyzed along with the details of the obligation.

Source and Importance of the Mitzvah

Torah Source

And it shall be for you a sign on your arm and a remembrance between your eyes so that the words of G-d be in your mouth, for G-d took you out of Egypt with a strong arm (Shmos 13:9).

And it shall be a sign on your arm and *totafos* **between your eyes, for G-d took you out of Egypt with a strong arm** (Shmos 13:16).

Bind them as a sign on your arm, and they shall be a *totafos* **between your eyes** (Devarim 6:8).

Bind them as a sign on your arms, and they shall be a *totafos* **between your eyes** (Devarim 11:18).

Reasons for Tefillin

The *Chinukh*, a classic fourteenth century text that attempts to explain the reasons for the various *mitzvos* writes:

"This *mitzvah* is based upon the fact that man, being a material creature, is drawn to his desires, since the nature of a material creature is to seek all that is sweet and pleasant, much as would a horse or a "brainless" mule. Only the Divinely given soul, commensurate with its strength, can prevent sin. Nevertheless, since it dwells in the body's habitat, earth, far away from its natural habitat, the heavens, it is relatively weaker than the body. It therefore needs, at the very least, many watchmen to protect it from its evil neighbor, who might otherwise kill it while under its (the body's) control. Since G-d wanted to give us, his holy nation, merit, he surrounded the soul with strong watchmen. These include the obligation to not cease studying Torah day and night, the four *tzitzis* fringes at the four corners of a garment, a mezuzah on our doorpost and **tefillin on our head and**

arms. All this is meant to remind us to refrain from using our hands for oppression and to not be led astray by our eyes and our thoughts."[1]

"The concept of these four *parshiyos* [in the tefillin] rather than any others is that these contain accepting the heavenly yoke of servitude, the unity of G-d and the idea of leaving *Mitzrayim*. This forces belief in creation of a world and the supervision of that world by G-d. Since these are foundations of Judaism, we were commanded to place these foundations between our eyes, and on our hearts. The eyes and the heart, according to those who know, represent the dwelling-place for the intellect, and by placing these things upon them to be remembered they reinforce us, we continue to remember the ways of G-d and we merit everlasting life."[2]

The Holiness of Tefillin

The *Rambam* writes that the holiness of tefillin is so great "that as long as a person wears them on his head and on his hand he will be humble and G-d fearing. He will neither be drawn into mockery nor into idle speech, nor will he dwell upon evil thoughts. Rather, he will open his heart to matters of truth and justice."[3]

Rewards and Punishment

"Tefillin are so important that whoever wears them lives long... is guaranteed a portion of the World to Come... is unaffected by the fires of Gehinom... and all his sins are forgiven. Whoever does not wear them is included in the [terrible] category of Jews who rebel with their bodies. As a result, all should be meticulous in fulfilling this requirement."[4]

A person should be at least as careful in his observance of the *mitzvah* of tefillin as with all the other *mitzvos*. The reason for this is that our sages said: "If never wearing tefillin is included among a person's sins, he is judged in accordance

1. *Chinukh* 421.
2. *Chinukh* 422.
3. *Yad Hachazakah, Hilchos Tefillin* 4:25.
4. *Tur, Orach Chaim* 37.

with his sins." The implication is that if he *does* wear tefillin, he is judged less stringently.[5]

The Obligation

Only men are obligated to wear tefillin,[6] from the day they turn thirteen, the day of their bar-mitzvah.[7] It is nevertheless customary to begin wearing tefillin before then to practice.[8] Some, however, begin only on the day of their bar-mitzvah.[9]

There are several customs concerning how much earlier to begin, including a week, two weeks[10], a month[11] two months and three months.[12] Each individual should follow the custom of his family.

When are Tefillin Worn

Tefillin are worn every day other than Shabbos and the holidays of Rosh Hashannah, Yom Kippur, Sukkos, Pesach and Shavuos.[13] Regarding the intermediate days of Sukkos and Pesach (*Chol Hamoed*), there are two customs[14]: Non-Chassidic Jews of European origin who do not live in Israel, wear it and either do not recite the blessing or recite it quietly. All others, including Chassidim, Sefardim, and all residents of Israel,[15] do not wear tefillin on those days.

---

5. *Or Haafelah* manuscript, cited in *Torah Shlemah, Bo* 13:118.
6. *Shulchan A'rukh, Orach Chaim* 38:3.
7. *Shulchan A'rukh, Orach Chaim* 616:2.
8. *Shulchan A'rukh, Orach Chaim* 37:3.
9. *Rama, Orach Chaim* 37:3. Many *Chassidim* follow this custom. Also see *Sheelos Utshuvos Yabia Omer* 6:3 for an overview.
10. The custom of some.
11. *A'rukh Hashulchan* 37:3.
12. *Mishnah Brurah*,37:12.
13. *Shulchan A'rukh, Orach Chaim* 31:1.
14. The *Shulchan A'rukh Orach Chaim* 31, prohibits wearing tefillin on *Chol Hamoed*, whereas the *Rama* requires wearing them. The *Gra, Orach Chaim* 31, supports the view of the *Shulchan A'rukh*.
15. See *Igros Moshe, Orach Chaim* 4:105.5 for the explanation why there is a universal custom in Israel not to wear tefillin on *Chol Hamoed*. He also writes that a visitor who wants to nevertheless wear them should do so only in the privacy of his room without reciting the blessing.

Tefillin are worn during the daylight hours only.[16] The specific time begins from the time that it is light enough to recognize a somewhat familiar acquaintance from a distance of close to seven feet,[17] and continues until sunset.[18]

Although the original requirement was to wear tefillin all day[19] (in fact that was the practice in Talmudic times[20]) the custom is to wear it for less time than that. The reason for this is that wearing tefillin requires a pure body, both physically (so that even venting wind is forbidden) and spiritually (so that a person's mind may not stray from the tefillin that he is wearing).This is all but impossible for most people.[21] Nevertheless, the minimum requirement is to wear it while reciting the *Shma* and the *Shmoneh Esrei* prayers.[22] The custom is to put them on before beginning the morning service[23] (after reciting the blessings of *Netilas Yadayim, Asher Yatzar* and the Torah blessings,[24] and after putting on the *Tallis*)[25] and remaining in them until after the service.[26] This is considered a short enough time period to be careful.[27]

16. *Shulchan A'rukh, Orach Chaim* 30:1-2.
17. ibid.
18. *Pri Megadim,* cited in *Mishnah Brurah,*30:3.
19. *Shulchan A'rukh, Orach Chaim* 37:2.
20. See *Bava Metzia* 105B, *Eruvin* 95B, *Beitzah* 15A et al.
21. *Shulchan A'rukh, Orach Chaim* 37:2.
22. *Shulchan A'rukh, Orach Chaim* 25:4 and 37:2.
23. See *Shulchan A'rukh, Orach Chaim* 25:2,3.
24. *Kaf Hachayim ,Orach Chaim* 25:68.
25. *Shulchan A'rukh, Orach Chaim* 25:1.
26. *Shulchan A'rukh, Orach Chaim* 25:13.
27. *Mishnah Brurah,*37:3.

A Note to the Reader

- This book is not meant to be an authoritative Halakhic work. Section I is a general explanation of the tefillin and its parts, without delving into the various stringencies and laws. Section II does deal with the *halakhos* of putting on tefillin, yet, it is not meant to take the place of the many excellent authoritative halakhic works on the subject. Similarly, it is not meant as a last word in situations of doubt. Rather, it is meant to impart knowledge to those who do not have the time to delve into the various sources on their own.

- The standard size print is reserved for the general descriptions and picture explanations. The small print is reserved for comments and sidelights. In Section II, the small print is generally reserved for technical advice and for customary stringencies. (It is worth noting that before changing the custom of one's family or accepting new stringencies beyond the requirements of halakhah, one should seek the counsel of a competent Rabbinical authority.) The color red that appears in the pictures is merely to emphasize specific subjects. Needless to say, that is not the real color.

Section One:

The Structure of Tefillin

Chapter One

The *Parshiyos*

At the heart of the tefillin are strips of parchment upon which are written four specific passages from the Torah. These are called parshiyos *(the plural of* parashah*).There are several differences between the* tefillin shel rosh *(the tefillin worn on the head) and the* tefillin shel yad *(the tefillin worn on the arm) in this respect.*

The *Tefillin Shel Yad Parshiyos* Four *parshiyos* on one strip.

פרשת "שמע"	פרשת "והיה אם שמע"
(דברים, ואתחנן, ו, ד-ט)	(דברים, עקב, פרק יא, פסוקים יג-כא)

והיה אם שמע תשמעו אל מצותי אשר אנכי מצוה אתכם היום לאהבה את יהוה אלהיכם ולעבדו בכל לבבכם ובכל נפשכם ונתתי מטר ארצכם בעתו יורה ומלקוש ואספת דגנך ותירשך ויצהרך ונתתי עשב בשדך לבהמתך ואכלת ושבעת השמרו לכם פן יפתה לבבכם וסרתם ועבדתם אלהים אחרים והשתחויתם להם וחרה אף יהוה בכם ועצר את השמים ולא יהיה מטר והאדמה לא תתן את יבולה ואבדתם מהרה מעל הארץ הטבה אשר יהוה נתן לכם ושמתם את דברי אלה על לבבכם ועל נפשכם וקשרתם אתם לאות על ידכם והיו לטוטפת בין עיניכם ולמדתם אתם את בניכם לדבר בם בשבתך בביתך ובלכתך בדרך ובשכבך ובקומך וכתבתם על מזוזות ביתך ובשעריך למען ירבו ימיכם וימי בניכם על האדמה אשר נשבע יהוה לאבתיכם לתת להם כימי השמים על הארץ

שמע ישראל יהוה אלהינו יהוה אחד ואהבת את יהוה אלהיך בכל לבבך ובכל נפשך ובכל מאדך והיו הדברים האלה אשר אנכי מצוך היום על לבבך ושננתם לבניך ודברת בם בשבתך בביתך ובלכתך בדרך ובשכבך ובקומך וקשרתם לאות על ידך והיו לטטפת בין עיניך וכתבתם על מזוזת ביתך ובשעריך

Tefillin Shel Rosh Parshiyos One *parashah* per strip

ויאמר משה אל העם זכור את היום הזה אשר יצאתם ממצרים מבית עבדים כי בחזק יד הוציא יהוה אתכם מזה ולא יאכל חמץ והיה כי יביאך יהוה אל ארץ הכנעני והחתי והאמרי והחוי והיבוסי אשר נשבע לאבתיך לתת לך ארץ זבת חלב ודבש ועבדת את העבדה הזאת בחדש הזה שבעת ימים תאכל מצת וביום השביעי חג ליהוה מצות יאכל את שבעת הימים ולא יראה לך חמץ ולא יראה לך שאר בכל גבלך והגדת לבנך ביום ההוא לאמר בעבור זה עשה יהוה לי בצאתי ממצרים והיה לך לאות על ידך ולזכרון בין עיניך למען תהיה תורת יהוה בפיך כי ביד חזקה הוצאך יהוה ממצרים ושמרת את החקה הזאת למועדה מימים ימימה

וכל פטר שגר בהמה אשר יהיה לך הזכרים ליהוה והעברת כל פטר רחם ליהוה וכל בכור בניך תפדה והיה כי ישאלך בנך מחר לאמר מה זאת ואמרת אליו בחזק יד הוציאנו יהוה ממצרים מבית עבדים ויהי כי הקשה פרעה לשלחנו ויהרג יהוה כל בכור בארץ מצרים מבכר אדם ועד בכור בהמה על כן אני זבח ליהוה כל פטר רחם הזכרים וכל בכור בני אפדה והיה לאות על ידכה ולטוטפת בין עיניך כי בחזק יד הוציאנו יהוה ממצרים

אלהיכם ולעבדו בכל לבבכם ובכל נפשכם ונתתי מטר ארצכם בעתו יורה ומלקוש ואספת דגנך ותירשך ויצהרך ונתתי עשב בשדך לבהמתך ואכלת ושבעת השמרו לכם פן יפתה לבבכם וסרתם ועבדתם אלהים אחרים והשתחויתם להם וחרה אף יהוה בכם ועצר את השמים ולא יהיה מטר והאדמה לא תתן את יבולה ואבדתם מהרה מעל הארץ הטבה אשר יהוה נתן לכם ושמתם את דברי אלה על לבבכם ועל נפשכם וקשרתם אתם לאות על ידכם והיו לטוטפת בין עיניכם ולמדתם אתם את בניכם לדבר בם בשבתך בביתך ובלכתך בדרך ובשכבך ובקומך וכתבתם על מזוזות ביתך ובשעריך למען ירבו ימיכם וימי בניכם על האדמה אשר נשבע יהוה לאבתיכם לתת להם כימי השמים על הארץ

פרשת "קדש לי"
(שמות, בא, פרק יג, פסוקים א-י)

פרשת "והיה כי ינ
(שמות, בא, פרק יג, פסוק

פרשת "קדש לי"

וידבר ידוד אל משה לאמר קדש לי כל בכור פטר כל רחם בבני ישראל באדם ובבהמה לי הוא ויאמר משה אל העם זכור את היום הזה אשר יצאתם ממצרים מבית עבדים כי בחזק יד הוציא ידוד אתכם מזה ולא יאכל חמץ היום אתם יצאים בחדש האביב והיה כי יביאך ידוד אל ארץ הכנעני והחתי והאמרי והחוי והיבוסי אשר נשבע לאבתיך לתת לך ארץ זבת חלב ודבש ועבדת את העבדה הזאת בחדש הזה שבעת ימים תאכל מצת וביום השביעי חג לידוד מצות יאכל את שבעת הימים ולא יראה לך חמץ ולא יראה לך שאר בכל גבלך והגדת לבנך ביום ההוא לאמר בעבור זה עשה ידוד לי בצאתי ממצרים והיה לך לאות על ידך ולזכרון בין עיניך למען תהיה תורת ידוד בפיך כי ביד חזקה הוצאך ידוד ממצרים ושמרת את החקה הזאת למועדה מימים ימימה

פרשת "והיה כי יביאך"

והיה כי יבאך ידוד אל ארץ הכנעני כאשר נשבע לך ולאבתיך ונתנה לך וכל פטר חמר תפדה בשה ואם לא תפדה וערפתו וכל בכור אדם בבניך תפדה והיה כי ישאלך בנך מחר לאמר מה זאת ואמרת אליו בחזק יד הוציאנו ידוד ממצרים מבית עבדים ויהי כי הקשה פרעה לשלחנו ויהרג ידוד כל בכור בארץ מצרים מבכר אדם ועד בכור בהמה על כן אני זבח לידוד כל פטר רחם הזכרים וכל בכור בני אפדה והיה לאות על ידכה ולטוטפת בין עיניך כי בחזק יד הוציאנו ידוד ממצרים

פרשת "שמע"

שמע ישראל ידוד אלהינו ידוד אחד ואהבת את ידוד אלהיך בכל לבבך ובכל נפשך ובכל מאדך והיו הדברים האלה אשר אנכי מצוך היום על לבבך ושננתם לבניך ודברת בם בשבתך בביתך ובלכתך בדרך ובשכבך ובקומך וקשרתם לאות על ידך והיו לטטפת בין עיניך וכתבתם על מזזות ביתך ובשעריך

פרשת "והיה אם שמע"

והיה אם שמע תשמעו אל מצותי אשר אנכי מצוה אתכם היום לאהבה את ידוד אלהיכם ולעבדו בכל לבבכם ובכל נפשכם ונתתי מטר ארצכם בעתו יורה ומלקוש ואספת דגנך ותירשך ויצהרך ונתתי עשב בשדך לבהמתך ואכלת ושבעת השמרו לכם פן יפתה לבבכם וסרתם ועבדתם אלהים אחרים והשתחויתם להם וחרה אף ידוד בכם ועצר את השמים ולא יהיה מטר והאדמה לא תתן את יבולה ואבדתם מהרה מעל הארץ הטבה אשר ידוד נתן לכם ושמתם את דברי אלה על לבבכם ועל נפשכם וקשרתם אתם לאות על ידכם והיו לטוטפת בין עיניכם ולמדתם אתם את בניכם לדבר בם בשבתך בביתך ובלכתך בדרך ובשכבך ובקומך וכתבתם על מזזות

The Four *Parshiyos in the Torah*

פרשת "שמע"
(דברים, ואתחנן, פרק ו, פסוקים ד-ט)

שְׁמַע יִשְׂרָאֵל. יְיָ אֱלֹהֵינוּ, יְיָ אֶחָד: וְאָהַבְתָּ אֵת יְיָ אֱלֹהֶיךָ, בְּכָל לְבָבְךָ וּבְכָל נַפְשְׁךָ וּבְכָל מְאֹדֶךָ: וְהָיוּ הַדְּבָרִים הָאֵלֶּה, אֲשֶׁר אָנֹכִי מְצַוְּךָ הַיּוֹם, עַל לְבָבֶךָ: וְשִׁנַּנְתָּם לְבָנֶיךָ וְדִבַּרְתָּ בָּם, בְּשִׁבְתְּךָ בְּבֵיתֶךָ, וּבְלֶכְתְּךָ בַדֶּרֶךְ, וּבְשָׁכְבְּךָ וּבְקוּמֶךָ: וּקְשַׁרְתָּם לְאוֹת עַל יָדֶךָ, וְהָיוּ לְטֹטָפֹת בֵּין עֵינֶיךָ: וּכְתַבְתָּם עַל מְזֻזוֹת בֵּיתֶךָ וּבִשְׁעָרֶיךָ:

פרשת "והיה אם שמע"
(דברים, עקב, פרק יא, פסוקים יג-כא)

וְהָיָה, אִם שָׁמֹעַ תִּשְׁמְעוּ אֶל מִצְוֺתַי, אֲשֶׁר אָנֹכִי מְצַוֶּה אֶתְכֶם הַיּוֹם, לְאַהֲבָה אֵת יְיָ אֱלֹהֵיכֶם וּלְעָבְדוֹ בְּכָל לְבַבְכֶם וּבְכָל נַפְשְׁכֶם: וְנָתַתִּי מְטַר אַרְצְכֶם בְּעִתּוֹ, יוֹרֶה וּמַלְקוֹשׁ, וְאָסַפְתָּ דְגָנֶךָ וְתִירֹשְׁךָ וְיִצְהָרֶךָ: וְנָתַתִּי עֵשֶׂב בְּשָׂדְךָ לִבְהֶמְתֶּךָ, וְאָכַלְתָּ וְשָׂבָעְתָּ: הִשָּׁמְרוּ לָכֶם פֶּן יִפְתֶּה לְבַבְכֶם, וְסַרְתֶּם וַעֲבַדְתֶּם אֱלֹהִים אֲחֵרִים וְהִשְׁתַּחֲוִיתֶם לָהֶם: וְחָרָה אַף יְיָ בָּכֶם, וְעָצַר אֶת הַשָּׁמַיִם וְלֹא יִהְיֶה מָטָר, וְהָאֲדָמָה לֹא תִתֵּן אֶת יְבוּלָהּ, וַאֲבַדְתֶּם מְהֵרָה מֵעַל הָאָרֶץ הַטֹּבָה, אֲשֶׁר יְיָ נֹתֵן לָכֶם: וְשַׂמְתֶּם אֶת דְּבָרַי אֵלֶּה עַל לְבַבְכֶם וְעַל נַפְשְׁכֶם, וּקְשַׁרְתֶּם אֹתָם לְאוֹת עַל יֶדְכֶם, וְהָיוּ לְטוֹטָפֹת בֵּין עֵינֵיכֶם: וְלִמַּדְתֶּם אֹתָם אֶת בְּנֵיכֶם לְדַבֵּר בָּם, בְּשִׁבְתְּךָ בְּבֵיתֶךָ, וּבְלֶכְתְּךָ בַדֶּרֶךְ, וּבְשָׁכְבְּךָ וּבְקוּמֶךָ: וּכְתַבְתָּם עַל מְזוּזוֹת בֵּיתֶךָ וּבִשְׁעָרֶיךָ: לְמַעַן יִרְבּוּ יְמֵיכֶם וִימֵי בְנֵיכֶם עַל הָאֲדָמָה אֲשֶׁר נִשְׁבַּע יְיָ לַאֲבֹתֵיכֶם לָתֵת לָהֶם, כִּימֵי הַשָּׁמַיִם עַל הָאָרֶץ:

פרשת "והיה כי יביאך"
(שמות, בא, פרק יג, פסוקים יא-טז)

פרשת "קדש לי"
(שמות, בא, פרק יג, פסוקים א-י)

וְהָיָה כִּי יְבִאֲךָ יְיָ אֶל אֶרֶץ הַכְּנַעֲנִי
כַּאֲשֶׁר נִשְׁבַּע לְךָ וְלַאֲבֹתֶיךָ, וּנְתָנָהּ לָךְ:
וְהַעֲבַרְתָּ כָל פֶּטֶר רֶחֶם לַייָ, וְכָל פֶּטֶר
שֶׁגֶר בְּהֵמָה אֲשֶׁר יִהְיֶה לְךָ הַזְּכָרִים
לַייָ: וְכָל פֶּטֶר חֲמֹר תִּפְדֶּה בְשֶׂה, וְאִם
לֹא תִפְדֶּה וַעֲרַפְתּוֹ, וְכֹל בְּכוֹר אָדָם
בְּבָנֶיךָ תִּפְדֶּה: וְהָיָה כִּי יִשְׁאָלְךָ בִנְךָ
מָחָר לֵאמֹר מַה־זֹּאת, וְאָמַרְתָּ אֵלָיו,
בְּחֹזֶק יָד הוֹצִיאָנוּ יְיָ מִמִּצְרַיִם מִבֵּית
עֲבָדִים: וַיְהִי כִּי הִקְשָׁה פַרְעֹה לְשַׁלְּחֵנוּ,
וַיַּהֲרֹג יְיָ כָּל בְּכוֹר בְּאֶרֶץ מִצְרַיִם,
מִבְּכֹר אָדָם וְעַד בְּכוֹר בְּהֵמָה, עַל כֵּן
אֲנִי זֹבֵחַ לַייָ כָּל פֶּטֶר רֶחֶם הַזְּכָרִים
וְכָל בְּכוֹר בָּנַי אֶפְדֶּה: וְהָיָה לְאוֹת עַל
יָדְכָה וּלְטוֹטָפֹת בֵּין עֵינֶיךָ, כִּי בְּחֹזֶק יָד
הוֹצִיאָנוּ יְיָ מִמִּצְרַיִם:

וַיְדַבֵּר יְיָ אֶל מֹשֶׁה לֵּאמֹר: קַדֶּשׁ־לִי
כָל בְּכוֹר פֶּטֶר כָּל רֶחֶם בִּבְנֵי יִשְׂרָאֵל
בָּאָדָם וּבַבְּהֵמָה לִי הוּא: וַיֹּאמֶר מֹשֶׁה
אֶל הָעָם זָכוֹר אֶת הַיּוֹם הַזֶּה אֲשֶׁר
יְצָאתֶם מִמִּצְרַיִם מִבֵּית עֲבָדִים, כִּי
בְּחֹזֶק יָד הוֹצִיא יְיָ אֶתְכֶם מִזֶּה, וְלֹא
יֵאָכֵל חָמֵץ: הַיּוֹם אַתֶּם יֹצְאִים, בְּחֹדֶשׁ
הָאָבִיב: וְהָיָה כִּי יְבִיאֲךָ יְיָ אֶל אֶרֶץ
הַכְּנַעֲנִי וְהַחִתִּי וְהָאֱמֹרִי וְהַחִוִּי וְהַיְבוּסִי,
אֲשֶׁר נִשְׁבַּע לַאֲבֹתֶיךָ לָתֶת לָךְ, אֶרֶץ זָבַת
חָלָב וּדְבָשׁ, וְעָבַדְתָּ אֶת הָעֲבֹדָה הַזֹּאת
בַּחֹדֶשׁ הַזֶּה: שִׁבְעַת יָמִים תֹּאכַל מַצֹּת,
וּבַיּוֹם הַשְּׁבִיעִי חַג לַייָ: מַצּוֹת יֵאָכֵל אֵת
שִׁבְעַת הַיָּמִים, וְלֹא יֵרָאֶה לְךָ חָמֵץ וְלֹא
יֵרָאֶה לְךָ שְׂאֹר בְּכָל גְּבֻלֶךָ: וְהִגַּדְתָּ לְבִנְךָ
בַּיּוֹם הַהוּא לֵאמֹר, בַּעֲבוּר זֶה עָשָׂה יְיָ
לִי בְּצֵאתִי מִמִּצְרָיִם: וְהָיָה לְךָ לְאוֹת
עַל יָדְךָ וּלְזִכָּרוֹן בֵּין עֵינֶיךָ, לְמַעַן תִּהְיֶה
תּוֹרַת יְיָ בְּפִיךָ, כִּי בְּיָד חֲזָקָה הוֹצִאֲךָ
יְיָ מִמִּצְרָיִם: וְשָׁמַרְתָּ אֶת הַחֻקָּה הַזֹּאת
לְמוֹעֲדָהּ, מִיָּמִים יָמִימָה:

Parchment for the *Parshiyos*

Two sets of the four *parshiyos* are written on long narrow strips of parchment. The first set is for the *tefillin shel yad*, and the second set is for the *tefillin shel rosh*. The following are the differences between the two sets:

A **The *tefillin shel yad* parchment strip:**

- All four *parshiyos* are written on one long narrow strip.
- Seven parallel lines are engraved across the length of the parchment to help the scribe write in straight lines.

B **The *tefillin shel rosh* parchment strip:**

- There are four separate strips of parchment, so that each *parashah* can be written on a separate strip.
- Four parallel lines are engraved along each strip.

The Type of Parchment

The parchment strips are made from the hides of kosher animals.

Parshiyos can be written on two types of processed parchment: **Natural parchment**, i.e., directly onto untreated parchment, and **Treated parchment**, i.e., onto parchment that was first coated.

In practice, the coating could perhaps be considered an interference between the letters and the parchment, which is unacceptable. Furthermore, the coating may crack when the parchment is folded. This would destroy whatever had been written there. Accordingly, **natural parchment is preferred**.

Ink for the *Parshiyos*

A special black ink is used for writing the *Sefer Torah, Tefillin* and *Mezuzos*.

"*STaM* " is the acronym used to refer to these three. Hence the scribe (*sofer*) who writes these three is referred to as a *Sofer Stam*.

A | **Strips of Parchment for the *shel yad parshiyos***

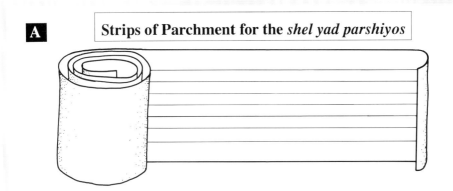

B | **Strips of Parchment for the *shel rosh parshiyos***

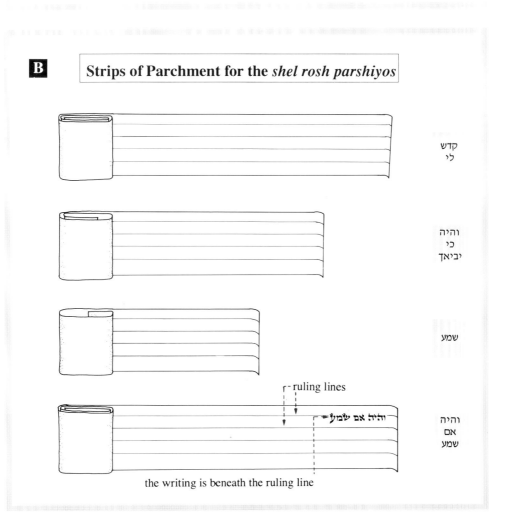

קדש
לי

והיה
כי
יביאך

שמע

ruling lines

והיה אם שמע

והיה
אם
שמע

the writing is beneath the ruling line

Types of Script for the *Parshiyos*

The *parshiyos* of tefillin are written in *Ashuri* script. This is the script reserved for Torah scrolls, mezuzos and tefillin.

There are two basic types of *Ashuri* script:

• Ashkenazi Script

Ashkenazi script is the script type used by Ashkenazi Jews. It is subdivided into two types: *Ari* **script,** which is customarily used by Chassidim, and *Beis Yosef* **script**, which is customarily used by non-Chassidim. The difference between these two scripts applies only to several letters (see the table below).

• Sefardi Script

Sefardi script is used by Sefardi and Yemenite Jews.

The Sefardi script on the facing page is the general style for Sefardi script, in accordance with the description of the *Mor Uketziah* (cited in *Kol Ya'akov*).

"*Velish* script" is an alternate name given to Sefardi Script.

The differences between *Ari* script and *Beis Yosef* (Ashkenazi) script							
שׁ	ץ	צ	ע	חח	ו	א	**Beis Yosef Script**
שׁ	ץ	צ	ע	חח	ו	א	**Chassidic (Ari) Script**

	כתב אשכנזי	כתב ספרדי		כתב אשכנזי	כתב ספרדי		כתב אשכנזי	כתב ספרדי
א	א	א	כ	כ	כ	ש	שׁ	שׁ
ב	ב	ב	ל	ל	ל	ת	ת	ת
ג	ג	ג	מ	מ	מ			
ד	ד	ד	נ	נ	נ			
ה	ה	ה	ס	ס	ס	אותיות סופיות		
ו	ו	ו	ע	ע	ע	ך	ך	ך
ז	ז	ז	פ	פ	פ	ם	ם	ם
ח	ח	ח	צ	צ	צ	ן	ן	ן
ט	ט	ט	ק	ק	ק	ף	ף	ף
י	י	י	ר	ר	ר	ץ	ץ	ץ

Chapter Two

The *Batim*

The batim *are the external housings for the* parshiyos. *They resemble cubes on top of squares* (titura), *which have an extra piece for the straps to go through* (ma'avarta). *There are many important details concerning how they are made.*

Batim

"*Batim*" (the plural of *bayis*) are the external housings of both tefillin. They are made from the tanned hides of kosher animals.

There are three types of *batim* : (**A**) *Gassos,* made from one strong thick piece of leather from a large animal (e.g., an ox); (**B**) *Dakos,* made from several pieces of leather that are covered with one piece of leather from a smaller animal (e.g., a goat or a ram); and (**C**) *Peshutos*, made from pieces of leather glued together. **In practice**: *Gassos* are to be preferred.

All surfaces of the *batim*, other than the bottom, are painted black.

The paint must be made from kosher ingredients only.

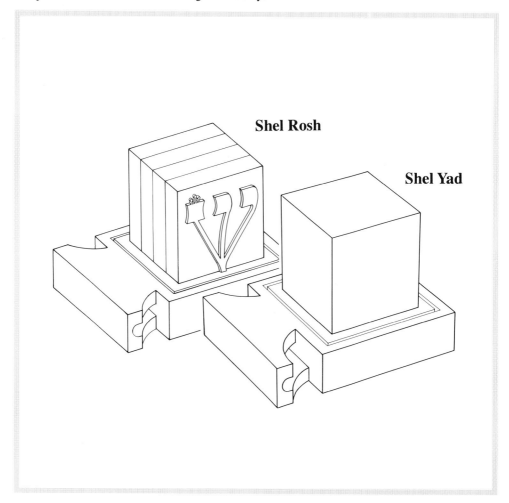

Parts of the *Batim*

The *batim* of both the hand and head tefillin have three main parts: The *bayis* cube, the *titura* and the *ma'avarta*.

Bayis cube is discussed on page 30, *Titura* is discussed on page 32 , *Ma'avarta* is discussed on page 34.

The *bayis* cube is generally referred to just as the *bayis*. The former term is used here to avoid confusion with the general term *bayis,* which refers to the entire external housing.

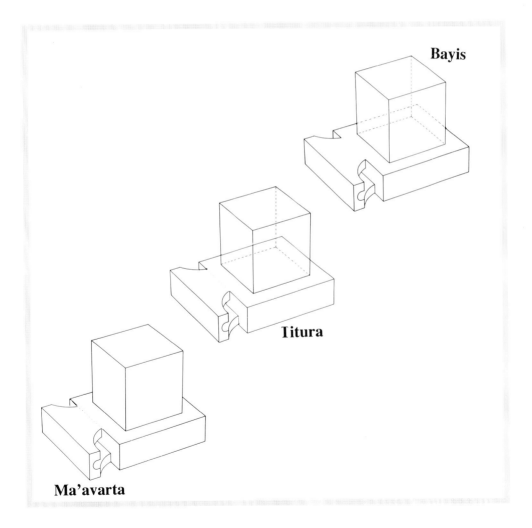

Bayis

Titura

Ma'avarta

Arm *Bayis* Cube

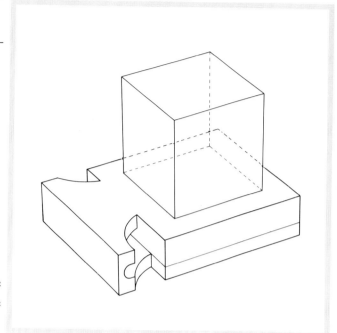

A single cube in which the *parshiyos shel yad* are placed.

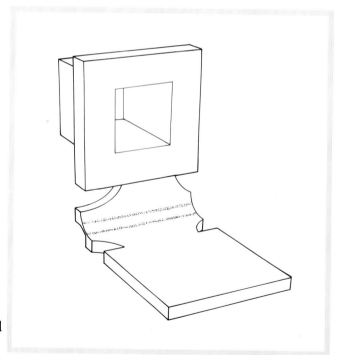

Internal view of an opened arm *bayis*.

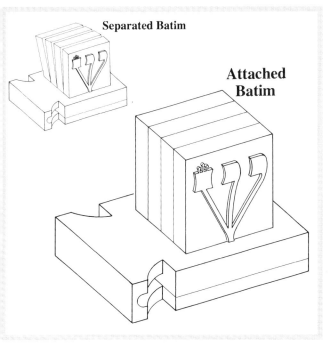

Separated Batim

Attached Batim

Head *Bayis*

Four separate sections of leather, each of which will contain one of the four *parshiyos*, are pressed together to form a cube.

In the early stages of preparation, the four sections are clearly separate parts of a single piece of leather.

Three grooves between the four sections must be visible so that four sections be clearly apparent.

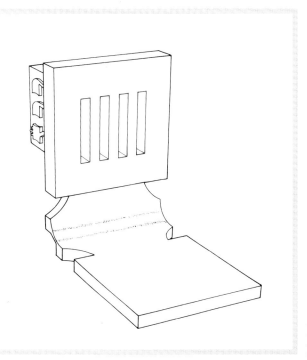

Internal view of an opened head *bayis*.

The *Titura*

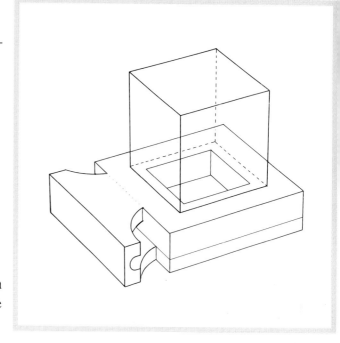

The square part beneath the *bayis* cube is called the *titura*.

The *titura* is composed of two separate parts:

1. The upper *titura*, which is the part that touches the *bayis* cube and has a square opening to match the opening in the *bayis* cube, and

2. the lower *titura*, which is the same size as the upper *titura*. It covers and closes the opening of the *bayis* cube.

It is called *titura*, which means bridge in Aramaic, because the lower *titura*, which covers the *bayis* cube, is reminiscent of the plank of a bridge.

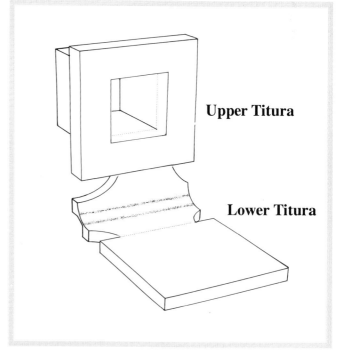

Upper Titura

Lower Titura

Titura Width

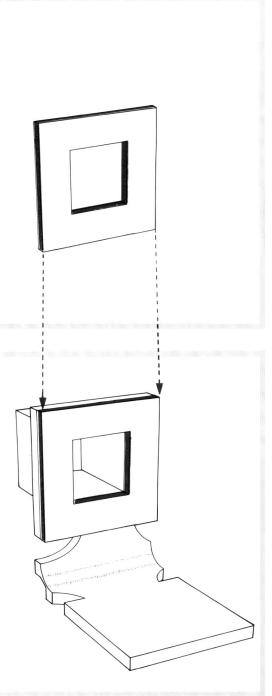

An additional square piece of leather is often attached to the upper *titura* to add thickness and strength to it. It has the same dimensions as the upper *titura,* with a central square hole of the dimensions of the *bayis* cube.

The square piece of leather attached to the *titura.*

This additional piece is only added when the leather of the *titura* is not thick enough in its own right. *Batim* whose leather is thick enough not to require an additional piece, are called *mikshah* (of one piece).

Ma'avarta

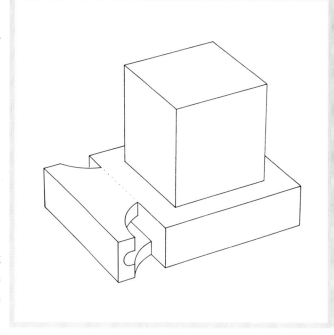

The part of the *bayis* that protrudes from the square *titura* is called the *ma'avarta*.

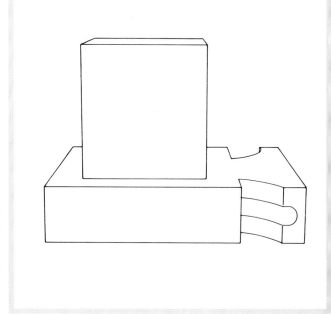

A hollow channel goes through the length of the *ma'avarta*. The strap is passed through (*ma'avar*) this channel. Hence the name *ma'avarta*.

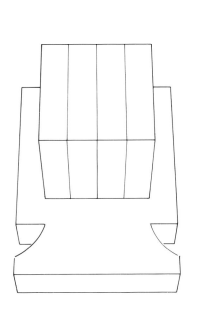

Ma'avarta Cuts

A quarter-circle niche is cut on either side of the *ma'avarta*, so that the shape of the *titura* can be perfectly square.

The squareness of the *titura* will be discussed on page 42.

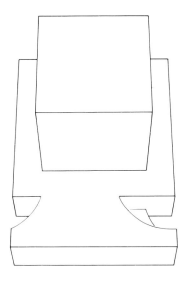

The right side of the *ma'avarta* on the *tefillin shel yad* has a larger cut , so that there be room for the knot of the *tefillin shel yad* strap.

The larger cut for a left-handed person is on the left side of the tefillin.

The *Shin* on the *Bayis Shel Rosh*

Two forms of the letter *shin* are written on the *bayis* of the *tefillin shel rosh*.

A. A Three-headed *Shin*

A three-headed *shin* protrudes on the right side of the *bayis* cube of the *tefillin shel rosh*.

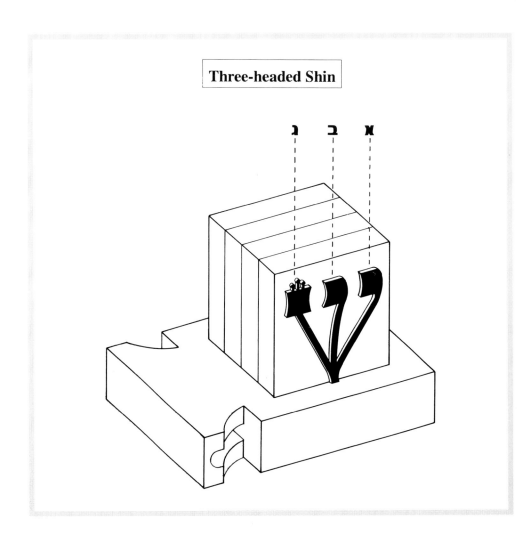

The *Shin* on the Head Tefillin (continued)

B. A Four-headed *Shin*

A four-headed *shin* protrudes on the left side of the *bayis* cube of the *shel rosh*.

Shin is the first letter of G-d's name, spelled *shin, dalet, yod*. See page 69 for an explanation as to how the entire name appears on the tefillin.

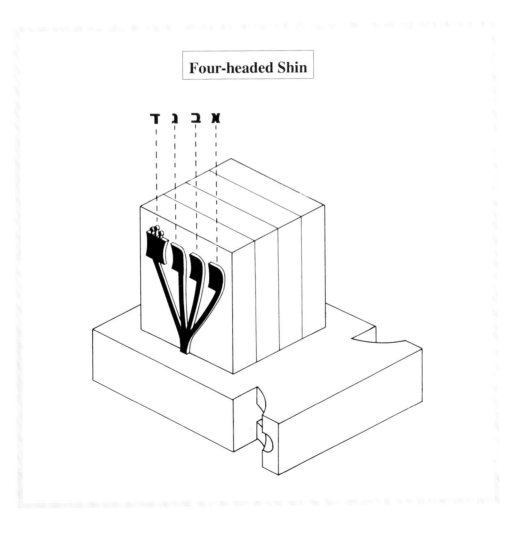

Four-headed Shin

Customs for the Shape of the *Shin*

Each of the three customs for *parshiyos* script that were discussed above, i.e.,

- *Beis Yosef* **script**, the Ashkenazi custom;
- *Ari* **script**, the Chassidic custom; and
- **Sefardi script**, the Sefardi and Yemenite custom,

has its own customary shape for these two types of *shin*.

Although it is customary for some to write this *shin* as it is written for the *parshiyos*, it is generally written differently. The bottom of the *shin* in the *parshiyos* slants to the left according to all three customs, whereas these *shins* end in the center. The central joining of all parts of the *shin* on the bottom enhances the beauty of the tefillin.

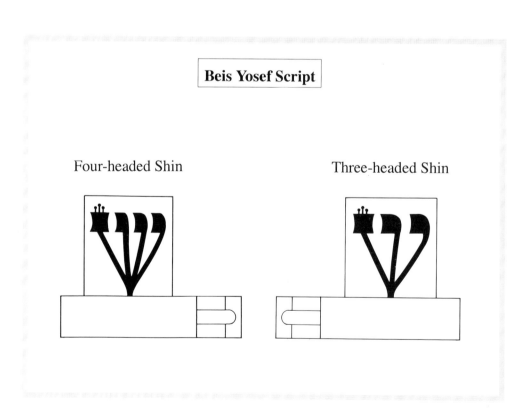

Beis Yosef Script

Four-headed Shin   Three-headed Shin

Ari Script

Four-headed Shin 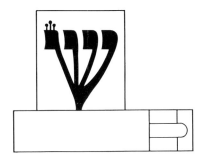   Three-headed Shin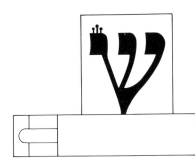

Sefardi Script

Four-headed Shin 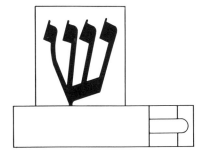   Three-headed Shin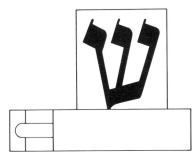

Sewing Holes

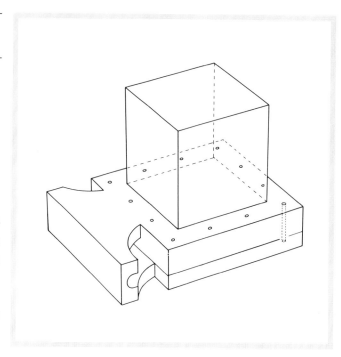

There are twelve holes spread around the *titura* through which thread is sewn to close the *titura* .

Sewing the *batim* is discussed on pages 54 .

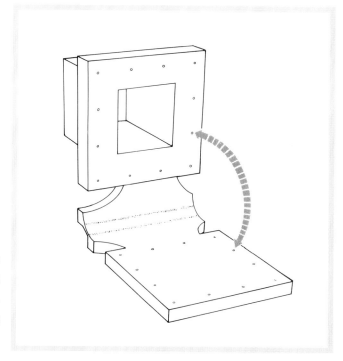

A view of the sewing holes in an open *bayis*. The holes of the upper *titura* are ex- actly even with the holes of the lower *titura*.

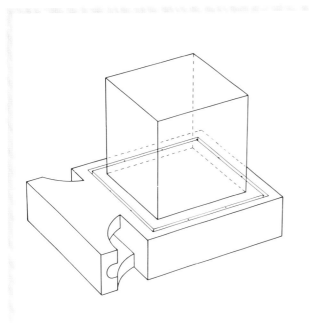

Sewing Slits

There are slits in the leather of the *titura* between each hole. The thread is meant to lie in these slits, thereby insuring that the thread forms a perfect square.

Squareness of the stitching is discussed on page 43.

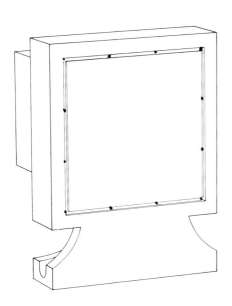

The sewing slits on the bottom of the *titura*.

Squareness

There are three square parts to tefillin:

A. Square *Bayis* Cube

The length and width of the cube must be equal.

The entire height of the cube must maintain its squareness.

A special protective covering is usually placed over the hand *bayis* cube. This prevents ruining the square as a result of friction from the sleeve or the like.

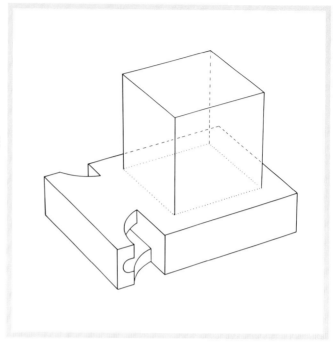

B. Squared *Titura*

The length and width of the *titura* must be equal.

The entire height of the *titura* must maintain its squareness.

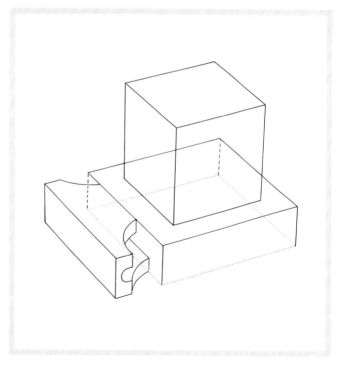

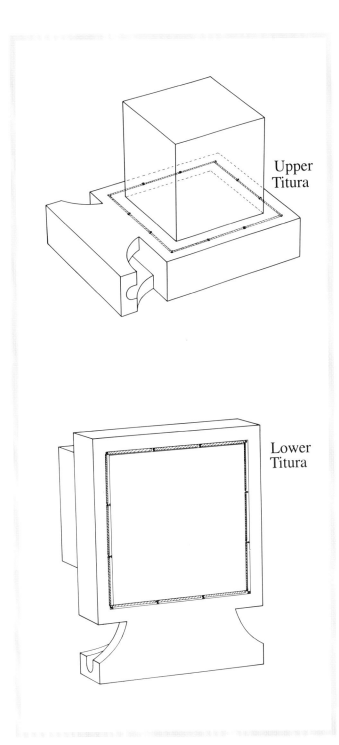

Upper
Titura

Lower
Titura

C. Squared Stitching

The stitching around the *bayis* cube must be squared.

This square stitching is visible both on the top and on the bottom of the *titura*.

The stitching is discussed on p. 54.

The Thread Between the Sections - Visible Parts

At the bottom of either side of the grooves that separate the four compartments of the *tefillin shel rosh*, pieces of the thread that passes through the sections are visible. This is an additional indication that the head *bayis* cube is truly separated into four sections.

Page 53 describes how the thread passes through the compartments.

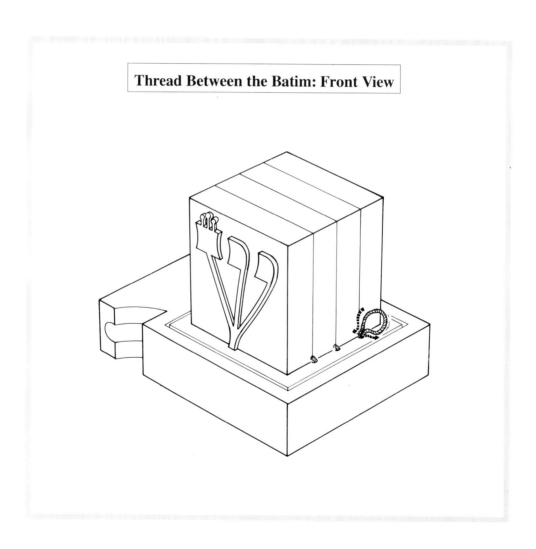

Thread Between the Batim: Front View

(continued)

This thread is made from the sinews of kosher animals.

It is sometimes difficult to see the thread when it is covered by the black paint used on the rest of the *bayis*. It is preferable that the thread be visible.

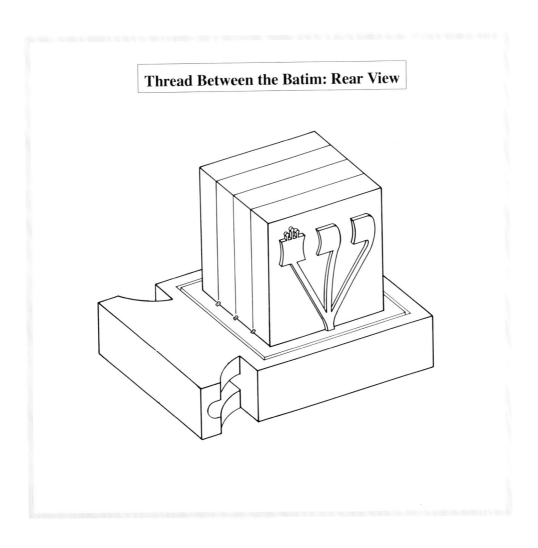

Thread Between the Batim: Rear View

The Thread Between the Sections - Unseen Parts

A **Channels:** On the bottom of the *bayis* cube of the *shel rosh*, there are three channels between the four compartments.

They are made as follows: **(A)** Steel thread is placed at the bottom of the compartments while the leather is still soft and moist. **(B)** The compartments are then compressed together. **(C)** The steel thread is left between the compartments as they dry. **(D)** The thread is removed after the leather dries, thereby leaving hollow channels between the compartments.

B **Holes:** There are six holes through the upper *titura*, three on each side, in front of each groove between the compartments.

C **Threading through the channels and holes:** Sinew threaded onto a needle is pulled through the channels and holes in a specific manner.

The thread must be long enough to pass through the channels and then sew the *bayis* shut. Sewing the *bayis* is discussed on page 54.

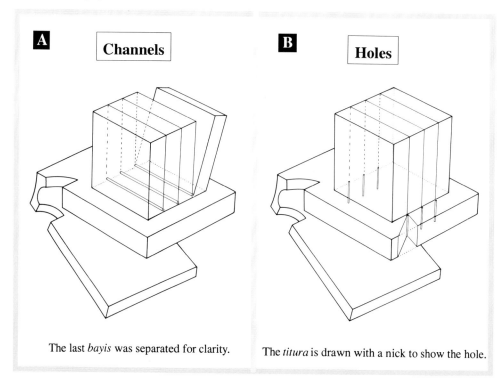

A **Channels**

B **Holes**

The last *bayis* was separated for clarity.   The *titura* is drawn with a nick to show the hole.

C | Threading Through the Channels and Holes |

end

beginning

The thread —An open view

beginning

end

Chapter Three

Placing *Parshiyos* into *Batim*

The parchment containing the parshiyos *must be folded in a specific way, tied with calf's hair, and placed into the* batim. *The* batim *are then sewn up with the remnants of the sinew thread described in the previous chapter.*

Folding and Wrapping the Head *Parshiyos*

The parchment for each *parshah* is individually folded so that it can fit into its own compartment. The following describes how it is folded:

A The parchment is folded over, close to an inch away from its end.

B The first piece is folded again and again over the rest of the parchment, resulting in a flattened "roll," unlike the cylindrical roll of the hand *parshah* (see p 56).

C Calf hairs (*se'ar e'gel*) are tied around the width (height) of the parchment.

D After tying the parchment, the hairs are not knotted. Rather, the ends are twisted together several times until they remain together and do not open.

E A thin strip of parchment is folded width wise over the hairs.

F Hairs of a calf are tied around this parchment strip as well.

G The hair ends are twisted together as in step D.

Folding the *parshiyos shel rosh* is discussed before folding the *parshiyos shel yad*, because the *parshiyos shel rosh* are placed into their *bayis* before the *parshiyos shel yad* are..

The hairs used to tie the parchment come from the tail of a calf. (When a calf is not available, the hairs from the tail of a cow or an ox may also be used).

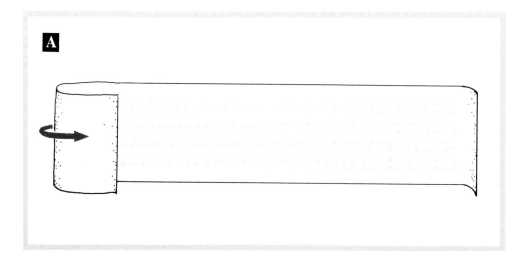

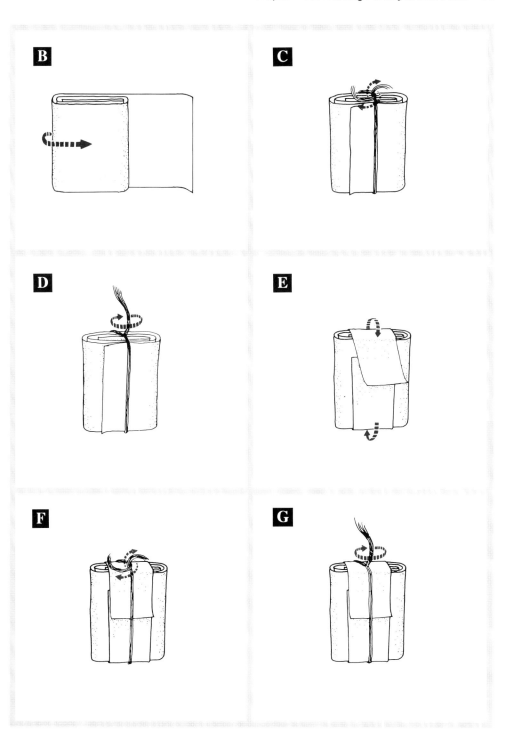

Placing the Head *Parshiyos* Into Their Compartments

After each *parashah* is folded, it is placed into its compartment as follows:

1. The *kadesh* *parashah* is folded and placed into the rightmost compartment.

2. The *vehayah ki* *parashah* is folded and placed into the next compartment.

3. The *shma* *parashah* is folded and placed into the third compartment.

4. The *vehayah im shamo'a* *parashah* is folded and placed into the leftmost compartment.

Longer calf hairs are wrapped around the *vehayah im shamo'a parashah*. See next page.

This follows the opinion of Rashi. See page 79 for the opinion of Rabeinu Tam.

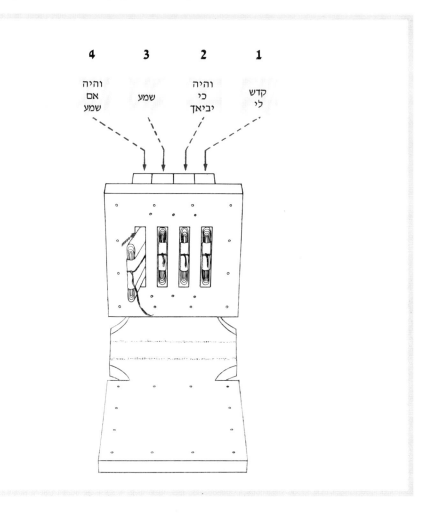

Extracting Calf Hairs Through the _Titura_ Hole

Some of the calf hairs must be visible externally. Accordingly, longer hairs are wrapped around the _"vehayah im shamo'a" parashah_ and their tips are threaded through a hole between the third and fourth compartments from the right.

This hole is one of the holes used to sew up the _bayis_. See p. 40 above.

This explanation follows the opinion of Rashi, see p. 79 for the opinion of Rabeinu Tam.

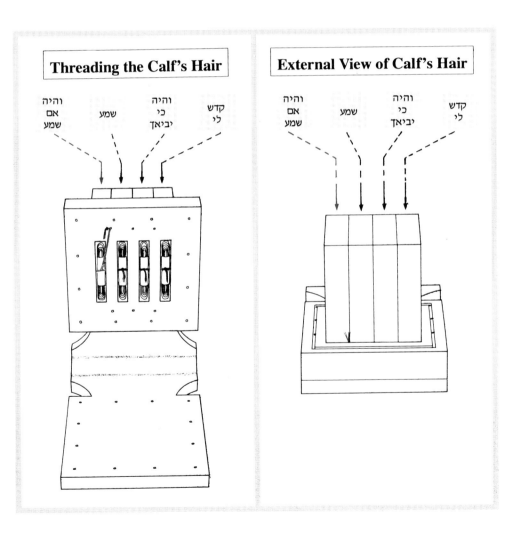

Threading the Calf's Hair

External View of Calf's Hair

The Sewing Thread

The continuation of the long sinew thread that had been threaded through the internal *bayis* (see p. 46) is used to sew the two parts of the *titura* together.

Some use a thread of ordinary length to thread through the internal *bayis*, and merely tie an additional length of thread to it for sewing the *titura*.

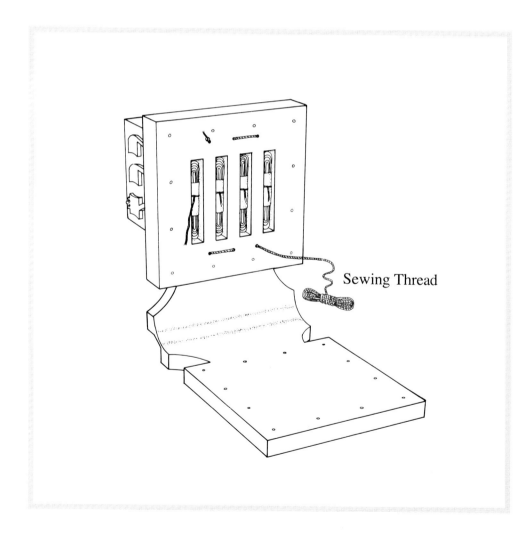

Sewing Thread

Sewing the *Bayis Shel Rosh*

The two parts of the *titura* are closed, and a needle with the sinew thread is used to pull through the sewing holes and sew the *bayis* shut, thereby sealing the *parshiyos* in their compartments.

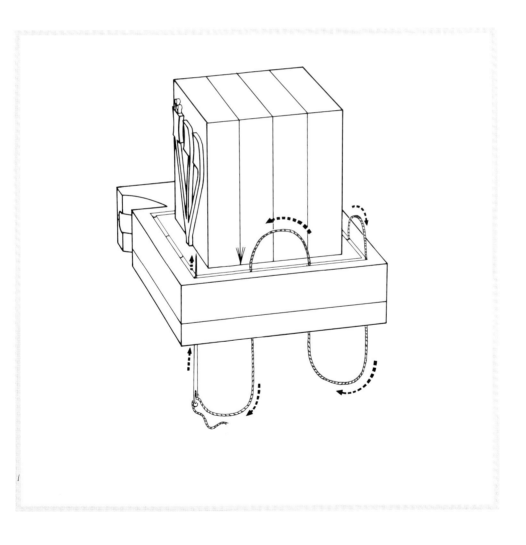

Rolling and Wrapping the Hand *Parshiyos*

Before placing the parchment containing the hand *parshiyos* into the *bayis*, it is rolled up and wrapped as follows:

A The end of the parchment is folded so that it begins to form a cylinder.

B The rest of the parchment is rolled up to its beginning, so that a cylinder is formed (unlike the flattened shape of the *parshiyos shel rosh*. See p. 50).

C Calf hairs are tied around the middle of this cylinder.

D After tying the parchment, the hairs are not knotted. Rather, the ends are twisted together several times until they remain together and do not open.

E A thin strip of parchment is folded width wise (top to bottom) over the hairs.

F Calf hairs are tied around this parchment strip as well.

G The hair ends are twisted together as in step D.

Some also tie calf hairs width wise (top to bottom) in steps C and E.

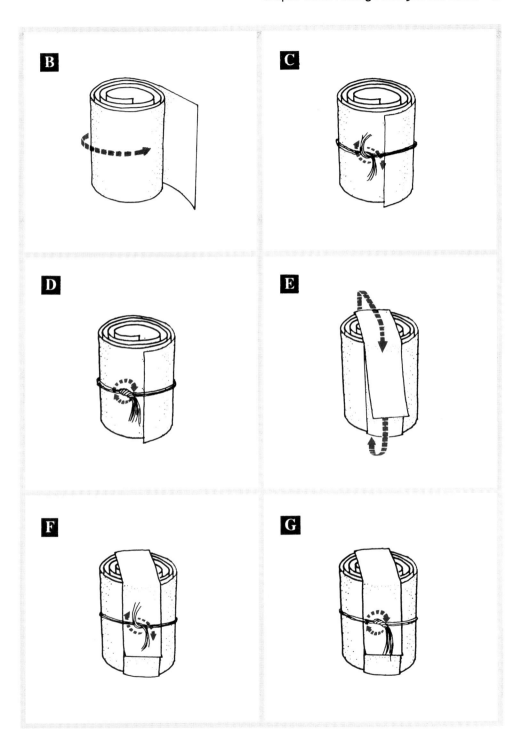

Placing the *Parshiyos* Into the *Bayis Shel Yad*

The wrapped *parshiyos shel yad* are placed into the hollow internal space in the *bayis shel yad*.

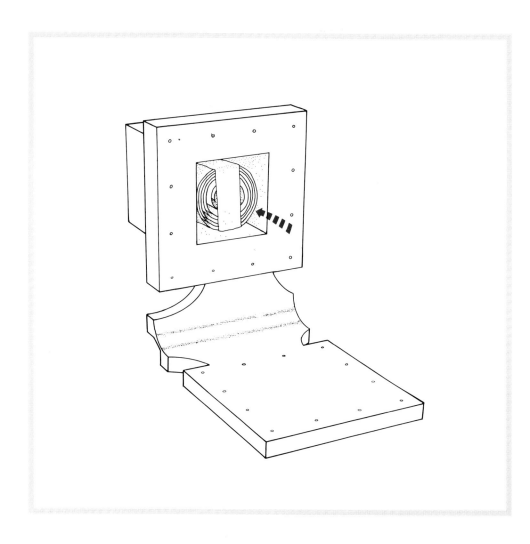

Sewing the *Bayis Shel Yad*

The two parts of the *titura* are pressed shut, and a needle with the sinew thread is used to pull through the sewing holes and sew the *bayis* shut, thereby closing the *parshiyos* in their *bayis*.

Sinew thread is a very strong thread that is made from the sinews of a kosher animal.

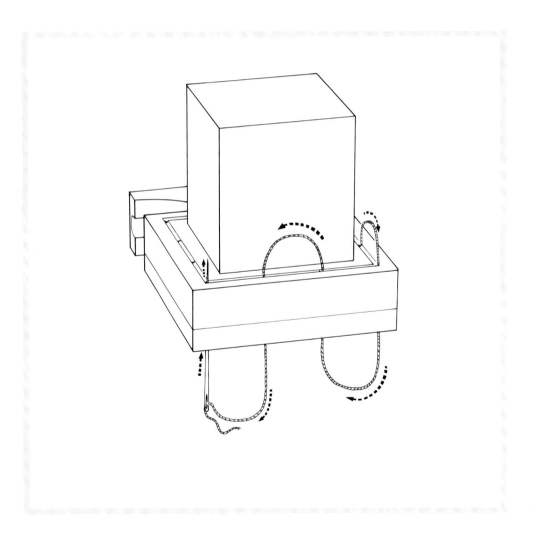

Chapter Four

The Straps and Their Knots

Leather straps are used to tie the hand tefillin to the arm and to hold the head tefillin on the head. The knots used to tie them to their respective tefillin resemble the letters of the name of G-d.

קשר תפילין הראה לעניו, תמונת ה׳ לנגד עיניו.

שיר הכבוד ״אנעים זמירות״

Straps

 Long thin strips of leather, *retzuo's*, are used to tie the tefillin to the arm and to the head. They are made of the processed leather of a kosher animal.

The smooth external side of the leather is painted black, and is referred to as the "black side." The rougher internal side is not painted, and is referred to as the "white side."

The black paint may not contain any derivatives of non-kosher sources.

Black Side

White Side

The Hand Knot

A knot, *kesher*, is tied on the strap of the *tefillin shel yad* so that a loop is left outside of it.

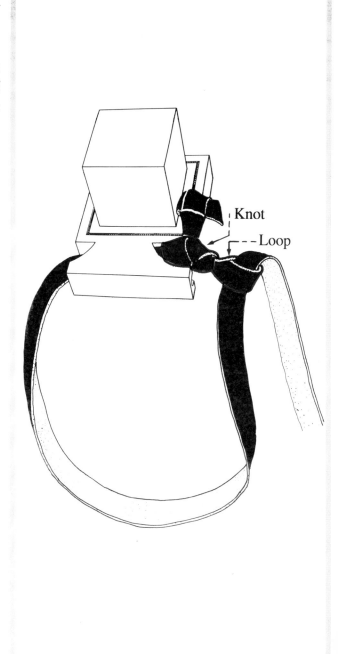

There are two customs concerning the location and size of the loop.

A. Ashkenazi Knot

A short loop comes out of the right side of the knot. The rest of the strap is pulled through this loop.

This is the custom of:

- Non-Chassidic Jews of European origin
- Chassidim of Polish origin
- Yemenite Jews.

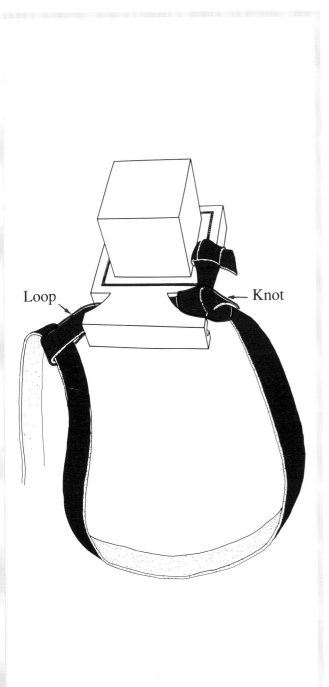

Loop

Knot

B. Sefardi Knot

A long loop on the left side of the knot is passed through the *ma'avarta*, so that a short loop emerges on its left side. The rest of the strap is pulled through this loop.

This is the custom of :
● Most Chassidim
● Sefardim

The Head Knot

A knot is tied on the strap of the head tefillin so that it can fit on a person's head.

There are two customs concerning the shape of this knot. In either case the Hebrew letter *dalet* is involved.

A. The *Dalet* Knot

The knot itself has the shape of a *dalet*, i.e., three out of four corners of a square knot.

This is the custom of:

- Most non-Chassidim of European origin
- Chassidim of Polish origin
- Sefardim

"Dalet" Knot

The "Dalet" shape is in the knot itself .

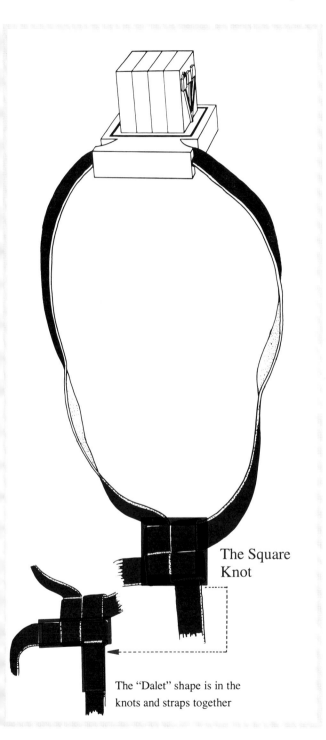

The Square Knot

The "Dalet" shape is in the knots and straps together

B. Square Knot

A square knot is tied and the Hebrew letter *dalet* is recognizable when looking at the knot and the straps together.

This is the custom of :

- Some non-Chassidic Jews of European origin
- Most Chassidim
- Yemenite Jews.

Some individuals tie a square knot containing a square space in the center.

Dalet is the second letter of the three-lettered name of G-d. See page 69.

The *Yod* of the Knot

The hand strap ends in two knots. The topmost knot is in the form of the Hebrew letter *yod*, which is referred to as the *yod shel hakesher* (the *yod* knot). The knot below it is the knot from which the loop, discussed above, emerges.

Yod is the last letter of G-d's name — *shin, dalet, yod* — which appears on the tefillin.

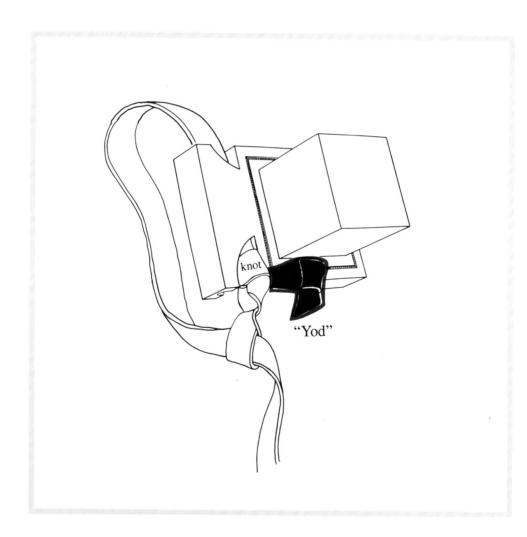

The Name of G-d on the Tefillin

Three Hebrew letters can be found on the tefillin:

- The letter *shin* (שׁ) on the sides of the *bayis shel yad*.

- The letter *dalet* (ד) on the *shel rosh* knot.

- The letter *yod* (י) on the *shel yad* knot.

These three letters spell out one of the holy names of G-d.

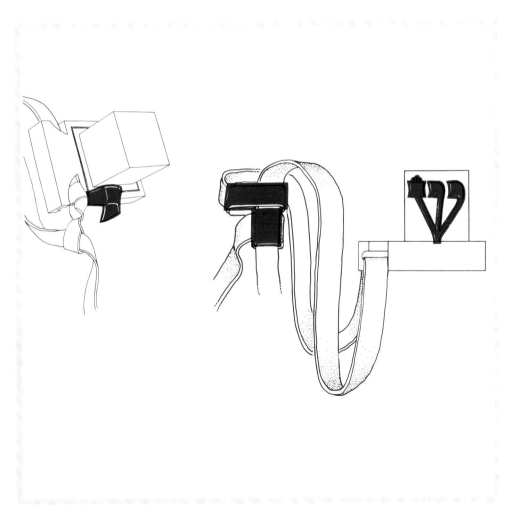

Chapter Five

Rashi Tefillin and Rabeinu Tam Tefillin

The tefillin discussed up to this point were made according to the customs attributed to Rashi. Rabeinu Tam, his grandson, followed an alternate ancient tradition. Certain individuals put on both kinds of tefillin. Tefillin made according to this custom differ in several important respects.

The Order of the Hand *Parshiyos*

The custom of Rashi and of Rabeinu Tam differ concerning the order in which the hand *parshiyos* are written on the single parchment strip.

According to Rashi: The order of the *parshiyos* (from right to left) is *kadesh*, *vehayah ki yeviachah*, *shma* and then *vehayah im shamo'a*.

This corresponds to the order in which they are written in the Torah.

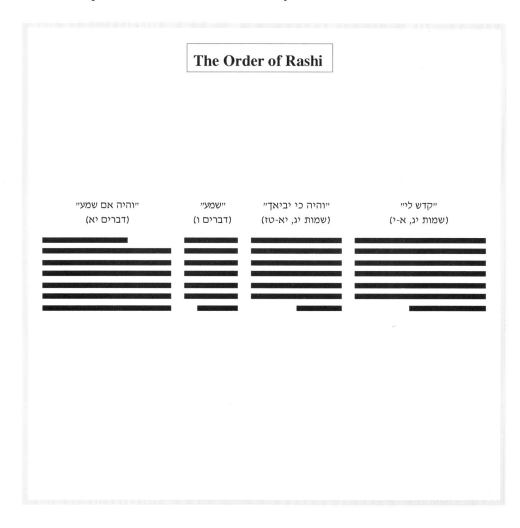

According to Rabeinu Tam: The order of the *parshiyos* (from right to left) is *kadesh, vehayah ki yeviacha, vehayah im shamo'a* and *shma*.

They differ with respect to order of the last two *parshiyos*.

There is no external way to differentiate between Rashi *tefillin shel yad* and Rabeinu Tam *tefillin shel yad*. Thus, once the tefillin are sewn up, they must be opened if necessary to check which type they are.

The Order of Rabeinu Tam

"שמע"   "והיה אם שמע"   "והיה כי יביאך"   "קדש לי"

The Order of Writing the Hand *Parshiyos*

Since the scribe is required to write the *parshiyos* in the order that they are written in the Torah, and since the two customs have different orders for the *parshiyos*, it follows that the scribe has to write the *parshiyos* differently for each custom.

According to Rashi: The four *parshiyos* — *kadesh*,[1] *vehaya ki yeviacha*,[2] *shma*[3] and *vehayah im shamo'a*[4] — are written one after the other, in the order that each is written in the Torah.

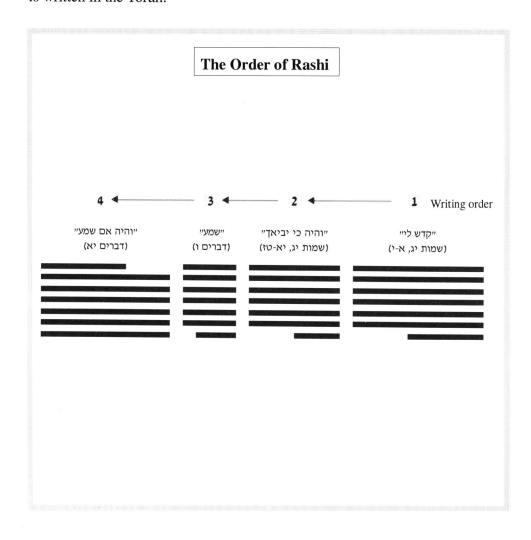

According to Rabeinu Tam: Since the order of the *parshiyos* does not follow the Torah order, the scribe must write the *parshiyos* in the following order:

A *Kadesh*[1] and *vehayah ki yeviacha*[2] are written in the normal order. A column for subsequently writing *vehayah im shamo'a* is skipped, and *shma*[3] is written at the end of the parchment strip.

B The scribe returns to the empty column and writes *vehayah im shamo'a*.[4]

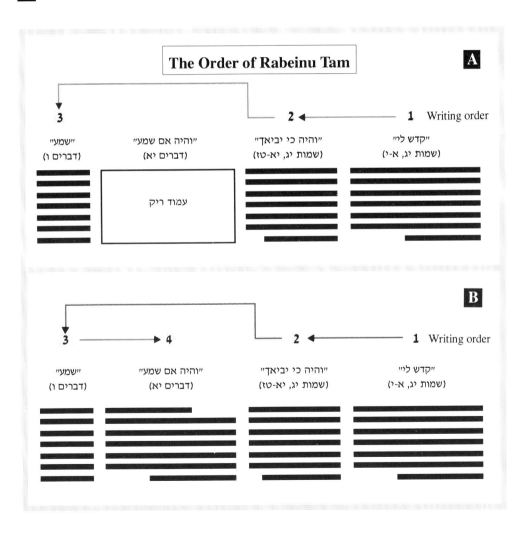

The Order of the Head *Parshiyos*

The two customs differ concerning the order of the *parshiyos shel rosh* as well.

According to Rashi: The *parshiyos* strips are placed into the *bayis* as follows: *Kadesh*, the rightmost; *vehayah ki*, next; *shma*, third and *vehayah im*, leftmost.

According to Rabeinu Tam: The strips are placed into the *bayis* as follows: *Kadesh*, the rightmost; *vehayah ki*, next; *vehayah im*, third and *shma,* leftmost.

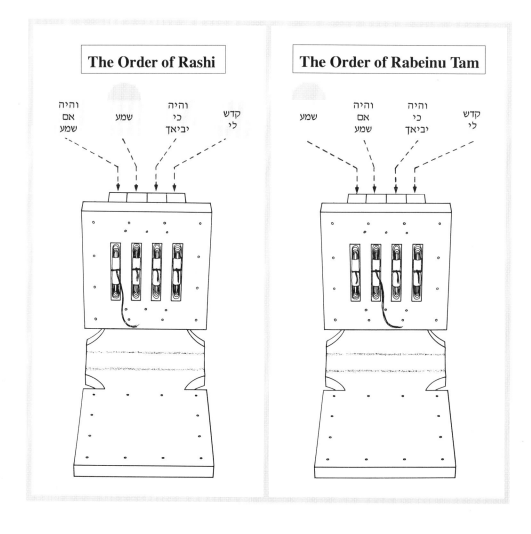

"Rightmost" and "leftmost" refers to the right and left of a person standing opposite another person wearing tefillin. What he sees on his right is the section containing the first *parashah*, and what he sees on the left is the section containing the last *parashah*.

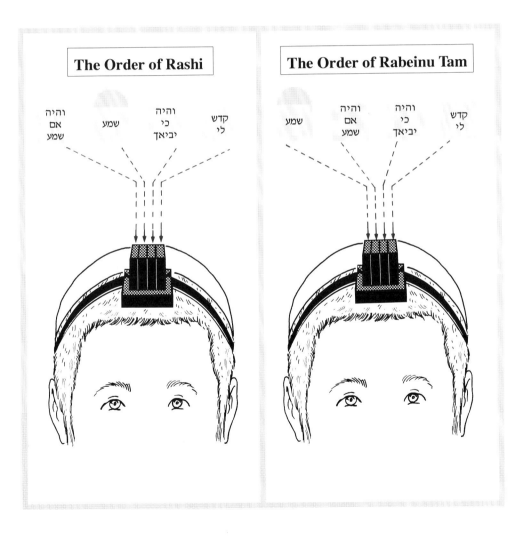

The Order of Rashi

והיה אם שמע שמע והיה כי יביאך קדש לי

The Order of Rabeinu Tam

שמע והיה אם שמע והיה כי יביאך קדש לי

Point of Emergence for the Calf Hairs

The calf hairs that wrap the *vehayah im shamo'a parashah* emerge to the right of that *parashah* (see page 53). As a result of the difference in placement of the *vehayah im shamo'a parashah*, the two customs also differ concerning this point. **According to Rashi:** Since the *vehayah im parashah* is the fourth from the right, the hairs are extracted from the hole between the third and fourth *parashah*. **According to Rabeinu Tam:** Since *vehayah im* is the third *parashah*, the hairs are extracted from the hole between the second and third *parshiyos*.

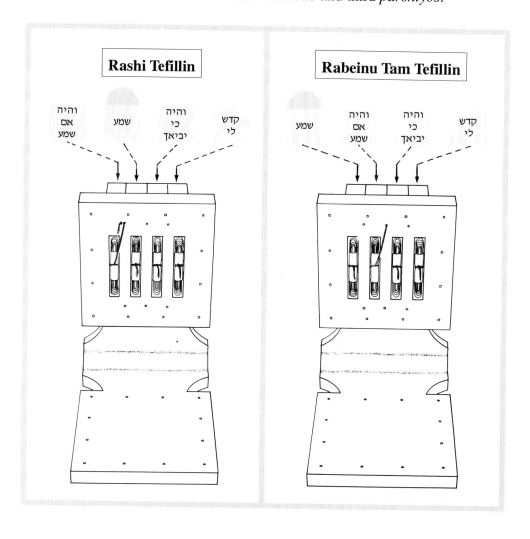

The position of the calf hairs is an external sign for differentiating between the tefillin of Rashi and of Rabeinu Tam even when the *batim* are closed.

In Rashi's Tefillin: The hairs protrude between the third and fourth section.

In Rabeinu Tam's Tefillin: The hairs protrude in the middle of the *bayis*.

In Practice: The *Shulchan A'rukh* rules that Rashi's tefillin should be worn. Those who follow the customs of the *Ari* wear Rabeinu Tam's tefillin **as well**, but do not recite the *brachah* when putting them on.

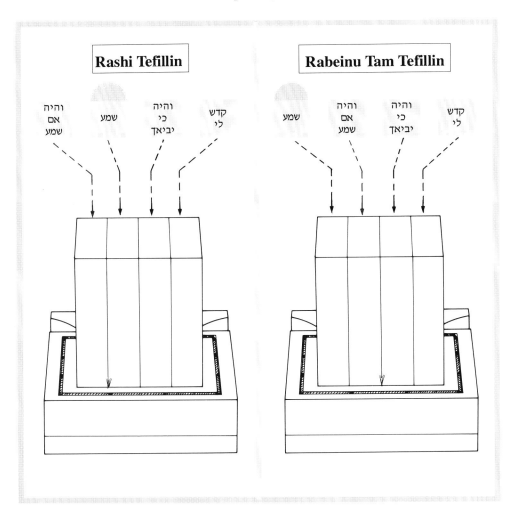

Schematic Summary

This mini-chapter will include a diagram illustrating all the sections of the tefillin shel yad, *a diagram illustrating all the sections of the* tefillin shel rosh *and a table summarizing the different customs relating to tefillin.*

A Summary of the Parts of the *Tefillin Shel Yad*

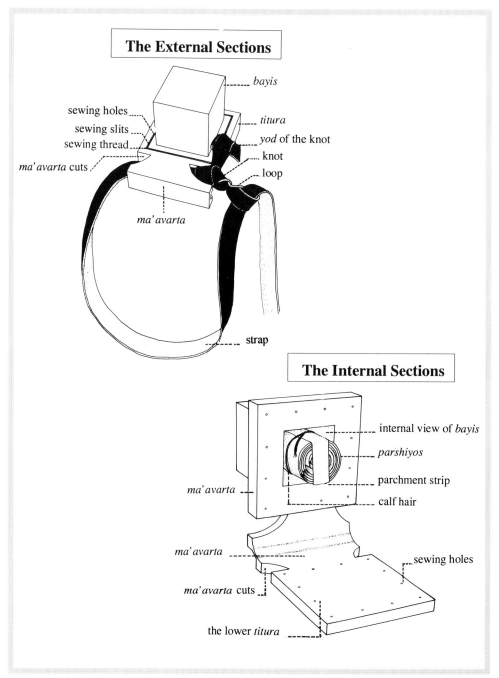

The External Sections

bayis

sewing holes

sewing slits

sewing thread

ma'avarta cuts

titura

yod of the knot

knot

loop

ma'avarta

strap

The Internal Sections

internal view of *bayis*

parshiyos

parchment strip

calf hair

ma'avarta

ma'avarta

sewing holes

ma'avarta cuts

the lower *titura*

A Summary of the Parts of the *Tefillin Shel Rosh*

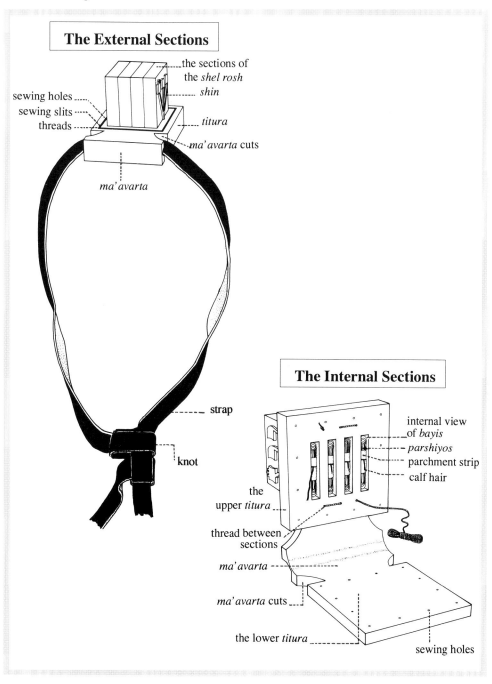

The External Sections

the sections of the *shel rosh*

shin

sewing holes

sewing slits

threads

titura

ma'avarta cuts

ma'avarta

strap

knot

The Internal Sections

internal view of *bayis*

parshiyos

parchment strip

calf hair

the upper *titura*

thread between sections

ma'avarta

ma'avarta cuts

the lower *titura*

sewing holes

A Summary of the Customs for Tefillin

Tefillin Part \ Group	Ashkenazim: General	Ashkenazim: Chassidic
Parshiyos: Script Type	*Beis Yosef* Script	*Ari Z"l* Script [1]
Batim: The *Shin*	*Beis Yosef* Script	*Ari Z"l* Script
Knots: *Shel Yad*	"Ashkenaz" — Loop faces the body	"Sefard" — Loop faces away from the body [1]
Knots: *Shel Rosh*	*Dalet* knot [1] Some use a square knot [2]	Square knot [3] Some use a *dalet* knot

Sefardim	Yemenite	Comments
Sefardic Script	Sefardic Script	1. Polish chassidim (not including Galicia) used to use Beis Yosef script, but they switched in Israel.
Sefardic Script	Sefardic Script	The *shin* of tefillin is generally (but not always) written slightly different from that in a Torah scroll.
"Sefard" — Loop faces away from the body	"Ashkenaz" — Loop faces the body	1. Polish Chassidim use an Ashkenaz knot – loop faces the body.
Dalet knot	Square knot Some changed to a *dalet* knot	1. Specifically those of Lithuania. 2. Those of Germany and W. Hungary 3. Such as Polish Chassidim.

Chapter Six

Concepts & Hidden Meanings

Over the ages many explanations have been presented for illuminating the concepts of tefillin. The following pages contain selected translations from these explanations.

Tefillin

Halakhah LeMosheh Misinai

From the written Torah we would not know the number of *parshiyos*, that there are four *batim* to the *tefillin shel rosh* and one for the *tefillin shel yad*, that there is a three-headed *shin* and a four-headed *shin*, nor that the straps must be black. All these are a tradition originating with Mosheh at Sinai (*Halakhah LeMosheh Misinai*).

Kad Hakemach of Rabeinu Bachye, Tefillin

The details concerning the shape, the *titura, ma'avarta*, squareness and stitches were transmitted from our fathers who received the information through the prophets person to person all the way back until Mosheh at Sinai.

Ramban, Shmos 13:16; *Tziyoni, Parashas Bo.*

Ten aspects of tefillin were *Halakhah LeMosheh Misinai.* Two refer to the way they are written and eight refer to the way they are housed and their straps.
The two concerning the way they are written:

- That they be written in black ink.
- That they be written on parchment.

The eight concerning their housing and straps:

- That the tefillin and its stitching be perfectly square.
- That the leather be *shin*-shaped on the right and left of the head tefillin.
- That the *parshiyos* be wrapped in cloth.
- That hairs be used to tie on top of the cloth before insertion.
- That they be tied with sinew thread.
- That there be a tunnel through which the strap can pass.
- That the straps be black.
- That they be knotted into a *dalet* shape.

Rambam, Tefillin 1:3 and 3:1.

Tefillin — A Miniature Holy Ark

The relationship between *batim* and the *parshiyos* is comparable to the relationship between the Holy Ark (*aron hakodesh*) and the tablets and Torah. They hold the *parshiyos* and protect them from the outside world. Thus, when the *parshiyos* command us to keep the entire Torah, the *batim* are a miniature Holy Ark.

Collected Writings of S.R. Hirsch

To this mission which has grown to us out of the exodus from Egypt and receiving the Torah each one of us is to make a "home", a *bayis*, a place for it to be realized and carried out, and moreover with squareness "by free-willed human activity" (as symbolized by being square; angles are not found in nature, only curves, angles denote human intentional work) and this "house", the *bayis* we are to create for the Torah is to have *titura*, is to have its "base", its basis on earth. Not in contrast to earthly matters, on the earth and with everything earthly it expects to be realized. And this base has its *ma'avarta*, it wants essentially to be borne by us, by human beings. It is nothing external, separated from our own personality from ourselves; it wishes to become true as part of ourselves, to make our own personal selves into a priestly consecrated Sanctuary of G-d. Like the Ark of the Covenant stretching its poles out towards the people, towards the nation, so do the tefillin, the Ark of the Covenant in miniature, stretch their *ma'avarta* out to every individual and say to him "bind yourself to me and bear me eternally through your life."

Hirsch, *Commentary on the Pentateuch, Devarim* 6:8 (I. Levy Translator)

Parshiyos

The *Parshiyos Shel Yad*

The *parshiyos shel yad* are written on one parchment strip and placed into one section to hint at the one G-d in His world. By wearing the *tefillin shel yad*, the Jewish nation, referred to as "one nation in the world," bears testimony to G-d's unity; the tefillin bear testimony that the wearer is a Jew who accepts all His commandments.

Reasons for Tefillin (by Rabbi Yom Tov Lipman Millhausen, Rabbi of Prague in medieval times) page 288

The *parshiyos shel yad* are written on seven lines to hint that G-d is very fond of the number seven, and to teach that G-d created the world in the merit of future keeping of the commandments related to seven. These include: Shabbas, the seventh day; *shemittah*, the seventh year; and *yovel*, which follows the seventh *shmittah*.

ibid

The seven lines of the *parshiyos shel yad* hint at G-d's dominion over seven heavens.

ibid, page 290

The *Parshiyos Shel Rosh*

A reason to support four lines on the *parshiyos*, four parchment strips and four sections to the *bayis*: The Torah uses the non-standard word *totafos* in reference to the head tefillin. The Talmud explains that each of the two halves of that word means two in a foreign language. The sum of the word is four, and hence the several fours related to *tefillin shel rosh*.

ibid, page 289

Parshiyos Shel Yad and *Shel Rosh*

The *parshiyos* of the tefillin represent the five books of the Torah. The four *parshiyos shel rosh*, written on four separate strips of parchment, represent the first four books. The *parshiyos shel yad*, written on one strip, represent *Devarim*, which includes the previous books (just as the hand strip includes all four *parshiyos*).

Sfas Emes, Bo, 5651

Why Were These Specific *Parshiyos* Chosen?

These four *parshiyos* were chosen above all others, because they contain the most basic principles of Judaism. They are:

- Accepting Heaven's rule
- G-d's unity
- The exodus from Egypt, which forces belief in a Creator who supervises the events of this world.

Chinukh, Mitzvah 424

Batim

A Three-Headed *Shin* and a Four-Headed *Shin*

The two types of *shin* correspond to the two scripts given at Sinai. The first, that of the tablets, was a "sunken script" in which the letters were inscribed into the walls. A *shin* written this way has four walls, as does the four-headed *shin* of tefillin, in which an ordinary *shin* is visible within the four raised parts of the *shin*. A three-headed *shin* is the ordinary *shin* written in the Torah, in which the raised ink corresponds with the raised folds of leather on tefillin.

Smag, cited by *Beis Yosef* 32; *Levush* 32, 43

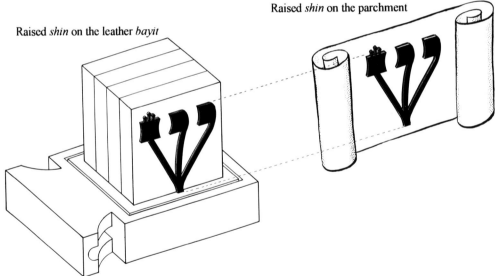

Raised *shin* on the parchment

Raised *shin* on the leather *bayit*

A Three-headed *Shin* representing the
Torah script – raised print on the parchment;
i.e., just as the ink of the *shin* appears raised from the parchment,
so too, the *shin* of the tefillin appears raised from the leather *bayis*.

To improve clarity, the *shin* on the parchment was made identical to the *shin* on the tefillin *bayis*. Actually, the Torah script is somewhat different from the illustration.

The four-headed *shin* is on the wearer's left and to the right of the observer before him. "The observer before him" refers to G-d, of whom it is written, "G-d is constantly before me" (Psalms 16:8). The four-headed *shin* on His right represents the *shin* sunken into the Tablets of the Ten Commandments, of which it is written, "From His right came a fire which became law " (*Devarim* 33:2). It is as if G-d said, "Put my *shin* to my right, and keep your *shin* [the shin used when writing the Torah] on your right."

Tikkun Tefillin, page 55

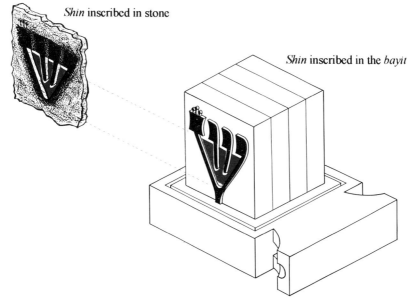

Shin inscribed in stone

Shin inscribed in the *bayit*

A Four-headed *Shin* representing the
inscribed script of the Tablets – script inscribed in stone;
i.e., just as the *shin* is sunken between the four walls of stone,
so too, the *shin* of the tefillin is sunken between four folds of leather.

The lower parts of the two central legs of the *shin* are connected on the tefillin that we wear.
They are not connected in the illustration to improve clarity.

A Three-Headed *Shin* and a Four-Headed *Shin* (continued)

The three-headed *shin* on a person's right represents the merit of our three forefathers, Abraham Isaac and Jacob. The four-headed *shin* on a person's left represents the merit of our foremothers, Sarah, Rebecca, Rachel and Leah. Thus, when a person wears tefillin, he has the merits of the forefathers on his right side, and the merits of the foremothers on his left side.

Baruch She-amar, 11

The three-headed *shin* on a person's right represents the three days of the week in which a portion of the Torah, given with the right hand, is read. The four headed *shin* on a person's left, represents the four days of the week in which a portion of the Torah is not read.

Baruch She-amar, 11

Two *Shins*

The importance of tefillin is so great that it is considered equivalent to all other commandments of the Torah. The numerical value of each *shin* is three hundred (300 x 2 = 600). Two *shins* together are read *shesh* which is Hebrew for six. Add three from the three-headed *shin* and four from the four-headed *shin* for a total of six hundred and thirteen, the number of commandments in the Torah.

Kad Hakemach, Tefillin

The *Shin* of Tefillin

The reason that specifically the letter *shin* is chosen to be written on the tefillin is to hint at the annual number of days in which tefillin are worn. The numerical value of *shin* is three hundred, which is the amount of annual days in which tefillin are worn. How so? The lunar year is normally 354 or 355 days, and it contains fifty Shabbasos in which tefillin are not worn. According to the original law of the Torah there was one day each of *Rosh Hashanah, Yom Kippur, Sukkos, Shmini Atzeres, Pesach* and Seventh day of *Pesach*, in which tefillin are not worn. The final total is generally three hundred, when you take into account that two or three of the seven holidays generally occur on Shabbas.

Levush 32,43

Placing the *Parshiyos* Into the *Batim*

Wrapping the *Parshiyos*

Why are the *parshiyos* wrapped in strips of parchment, tied with hairs and [sewn up wit] sinew? This hints at the resurrection when the Jewish dead will arise fully clothed, complete with their own hair, sinews and covered by skin. The body of the *parshiyos* (the written part) is comparable to the human body. The parchment upon which the *parshiyos* are written is comparable to human flesh. The sinews that sew the *parshiyos* up are comparable to human sinews and the parchment in which the *parshiyos* are wrapped is comparable to the clothing humans wear. This hints that whoever is G-d fearing and wears tefillin will merit the resurrection.

Kad Hakemach, Tefillin

Twelve Stitches

The twelve stitches on the head tefillin [which are worn "above"] hint at the twelve angels that surround the heavenly throne above. To correspond with that there were twelve tribes of Israel below that surrounded the Temple. They are hinted at by the twelve stitches on the hand tefillin [which are "below" with reference to the head tefillin.]

Kuntres Ta'amei Tefillin, p.290

The Straps

Blackness of the Straps

The blackness of the straps hints at the fact that a very deep matter is involved [and black represents the deepest of the colors.]

Rabeinu Bachye, Shmos 13:16

The color black is unique in that it will not show any other color mixed with it. This hints at the uniqueness of G-d. Accordingly, the *parshiyos* are written in black ink, and the *batim* and the straps are painted black.

Yafeh Lalev, 25:33

Black symbolizes something hidden, since blackness is equivalent to darkness. Just as darkness cannot be perceived, so too, this matter cannot be grasped. Others say that blackness hints at infinity.

Tziyoni, Parshas Bo

Why black? Because the reward for fulfilling the requirement of tefillin is being reborn at the end of days and appearing as a beautiful youth with the fully black hair of youth.

Pirush Harokeach al Hatorah, Vaeschanan

The *batim* have to also be black to hint at the Torah itself, which was written with black fire on white fire.

Tziyoni, Parshas Bo

Rashi and Rabeinu Tam Tefillin

This as Well as That is the Living Words of G-d

My question concerning the order of the *parshiyos* of tefillin was as follows:
Oh great, mighty and awesome King; Master of all that is secret; Revealer of
that which is hidden; Preserver of the covenant and all kindness; increase your
kindness to us today and command your holy angels to teach me the correct
order for the *parshiyos* of tefillin. Some authorities say that the tefillin are only
kosher if the *havayos*, the two *parshiyos* beginning *vehayah*, [*havayos* is also a
plural form of the sacred four-lettered name of G-d] are in the middle. Others
say that the tefillin are only kosher if the *havayos* follow the order that they are
written in the Torah. And now, King of Kings, command your holy angels to
reveal to me which view you prefer? Their reply was: This as well as that is the
living words of G-d. We dispute the same point up here. The Holy One, Blessed
Be He, says that *havayos* should be in the middle. All the rest of the Heavenly
community, however, says that *havayos* should be in order. This is the meaning
of His own words: "With the close to Me I shall be sanctified, and I shall be
honored in the face of the entire nation." It is in His honor that the *parashah* of
accepting the rulership of Heaven [*Shma'*] precede the others.

She-elos Utshuvos Min Hashamayim, 3

[The questions and answers took place in Divine dreams]

שמע	והיה אם שמע	והיה כי יביאך	קדש לי	***Havayos* in the Middle** The two "*vehayah*" *parshiyos* in the center of four *parshiyos*. (According to Rabeinu Tam)
והיה אם שמע (דברים)	שמע	והיה כי יביאך (שמות)	קדש לי	***Havayos* in Order** The two "*vehayah*" *parshiyos* follow the Torah's order. (According to Rashi)

The Torah writes that when Yosef saw his father place his right hand on the head of Ephraim, Yosef's younger son, and the left hand on the head of Menasheh his eldest, he said, "Not so, father, for he [Menasheh] is the eldest..." (*Breishis* 48:18). The disagreement between them was as follows: Yosef, as the choicest of the brothers, whose service of G-d was totally free of any impurity, saw these qualities in Menasheh, and felt that he therefore deserved the primary blessings. Ya'akov, on the other hand, understood that most people could not be so totally free of impurities, and thus gave the primary blessing to Ephraim.... This is also the underlying difference between the tefillin of Rashi and Rabeinu Tam. The *parshiyos* in the tefillin of Rashi follow the order in which they were written in the Torah, *Shma*, which represents accepting the heavenly yoke, preceding *Vehayah Im Shamo'a*, which represents accepting the yoke of the mitzvos. On the other hand, *Shma'* is the last *parashah* in the tefillin of Rabeinu Tam. This represents accepting the yoke of heaven as a last step, after having been fully purified in all other aspects. Those who understood the secret Truths wrote that the tefillin of Rabeinu Tam represent a higher level than the tefillin of Rashi, for it represents a more difficult way to serve G-d.

Sfas Emes, Siddur, page 37

Section Two:

How to Put On Tefillin

Chapter Seven

Before Putting On the Tefillin

Several points should be known before putting on the tefillin. These include:

A. The location at which one should be when putting them on,

B. The physical preparations that are required,

C. The preparatory prayer that is recited.

The Location for Putting on Tefillin

The *Shulchan A'rukh* rules that the *tallis* and tefillin should be put on at home so that one may walk to the synagogue adorned by them.[1] The later authorities add that if it is difficult to walk through the streets wearing a *tallis* and tefillin they should be put on before entering the synagogue proper, in a side room or in the courtyard before the synagogue.[2]

When they cannot be put on before entering the synagogue, they may be put on in the synagogue itself.[3]

One should try to put the tefillin on near a comfortable roomy surface such as a table. This prevents the tefillin from falling down as they are being put on, and helps avoid dragging the straps on the ground as they are unwound.[4]

One should avoid putting the tefillin onto narrow sloped surfaces from which they can easily fall. (If the tefillin nevertheless fall, but are still in the tefillin bag, a small donation should be given to charity.)[5] Similarly, one should not put tefillin on in a busy aisle, to prevent the possibility of the tefillin being pushed out of his hands.

The tefillin bag should not be put down with the bottom side up.[6]

Those who follow the Sefardi custom of putting tefillin on while seated, should be careful not to sit on a bench containing tefillin. If the only place available for placing the tefillin is the bench upon which he will sit, he may place the tefillin on top of an object on the bench that is at least 8 centimeters[7] (a bit over 3 inches) high.[8] If such an object is unavailable, he may nevertheless sit on the bench, provided that the tefillin are on top of the tefillin bag rather than directly on the bench.[9]

1   *Shulchan A'rukh* and *Rama*, 25:2.
2   *Mishnah Brurah* 25:8; *Olas Tamid* 25:3; *Kaf Hachayim* 25:16.
3   See *A'rukh Hashulchan* 25:2.
4   *Kitzur Shelah, Hilchos Tefillin; A'rukh Hashulchan,*40:1.
5   *Mishnah Brurah* 40:3.
6   See *Elyah Rabah* 40:5.
7   The measurements of Rabbi Chaim Naeh, followed by the Sefardim.
8   *Tshuvos Haradbaz* III, end of 515 (950).
9   See *Chayei Adam* 31:43; *Misgeres Hashulchan* 40:1.

The Physical Preparations

Check the following before putting on tefillin:

- That your body is clean internally (i.e. no urge to go to the bathroom) and externally.[10]

- Whether your arm or head is wet from water or perspiration. If so, dry the wet area thoroughly before putting on tefillin. The reason for this is that it is not respectful to place the tefillin on water or perspiration.[11] In addition, water might be considered a barrier between your skin and the tefillin[12] (perspiration is not considered a barrier[13]). Furthermore, wetness can cause the tefillin to warp which can possibly render them non-kosher.

- Whether there is any dirt such as dust or dried paint that would cause a barrier between the tefillin and your arm. If such a barrier exists anywhere along the area that the tefillin are placed and the straps are wound, it should be removed before putting the tefillin on.[14]

- If you wear a wrist watch upon the arm on which the tefillin will be placed, it is highly preferable to remove the watch before putting on the tefillin.[15]

---

10 See *Shulchan A'rukh* 38:2.
11 *Od Yosef Chai, Vayera* 19. He writes that perspiration after putting the tefillin on is not a problem. See also *Kaf Hachayim* 27:16.
12 *Kaf Hachayim op cit*. According to *Os Chayim Veshalom*, water on the arm is considered a barrier, as opposed to perspiration on the head which is not.
13 *Od Yosef Chai, Vayera* 19.
14 See *Shulchan A'rukh* 27:4; *Mishnah Brurah* 27:14; *Kaf Hachayim* 27:20.
15 *Beis Barukh* 14:93. See *Yalkut Yosef Hilkhos Tefillin* 4, who writes that in principle it is permitted to wind the tefillin straps on top of a watch, which is not considered a barrier provided that the strap is wound seven times before that. However, he concludes that those who are stricter should be blessed. He also writes that although *Dovev Meisharim* II:37 requires removing the watch, he later changed his mind.

The Prayer Before Putting on Tefillin

It is customary to recite a special prayer[16] before putting on the tefillin. There are four parts to the prayer: **A.** Affirming the unity of G-d, **B.** The intention to fulfill the commandment of putting on tefillin,[17]   **C.** First request.   **D.** Second request. The following is the prayer in Hebrew and in English:

A. Affirming G-d's Unity:

For the sake of unifying the Holy One Blessed Be He and His Presence, with fear and love to unify the Divine four-lettered Name in perfect unity, in the name of all Israel.

• יְחוּד הַשֵּׁם: לְשֵׁם יְחוּד קוּדְשָׁא בְּרִיךְ הוּא וּשְׁכִינְתֵּהּ בִּדְחִילוּ וּרְחִימוּ לְיַחֵד שֵׁם י"ה בּו"ה בְּיִחוּדָא שְׁלִים בְּשֵׁם כָּל יִשְׂרָאֵל.

B. Intention to Fulfill:

My intention in putting on tefillin is to fulfill the commandment of our Creator who commanded us to put on tefillin, as is written in His Torah: "Tie them as a sign upon your arm and let them be *totafos* between your eyes." They include four portions: *Shma, Vehayah im shamo'a, Kadesh* and *Vehayah ki yeviachah*, which contain His Oneness and Unity, may His Name be blessed in the world, in order that we remember the miracles and wonders that He did for us when taking us out of Egypt, and He has the strength and power over all above

• כַּוָּנַת מִצְוַת הֲנָחַת תְּפִילִין[17]: הִנְנִי מְכַוֵּן בַּהֲנָחַת תְּפִלִּין לְקַיֵּם מִצְוַת בּוֹרְאֵנוּ, שֶׁצִּוָּנוּ לְהָנִיחַ תְּפִלִּין, כַּכָּתוּב בַּתּוֹרָה: וּקְשַׁרְתָּם לְאוֹת עַל יָדֶךָ, וְהָיוּ לְטֹטָפֹת בֵּין עֵינֶיךָ, וְהֵן אַרְבַּע פָּרָשִׁיּוֹת אֵלּוּ: שְׁמַע, וְהָיָה אִם שָׁמֹעַ, קַדֶּשׁ, וְהָיָה כִּי יְבִיאֲךָ, שֶׁיֵּשׁ בָּהֶם יִחוּדוֹ וְאַחְדּוּתוֹ יִתְבָּרַךְ שְׁמוֹ בָּעוֹלָם, וְשֶׁנִּזְכֹּר נִסִּים וְנִפְלָאוֹת, שֶׁעָשָׂה עִמָּנוּ בְּהוֹצִיאָנוּ מִמִּצְרַיִם, וַאֲשֶׁר לוֹ הַכֹּחַ וְהַמֶּמְשָׁלָה בָּעֶלְיוֹנִים וּבַתַּחְתּוֹנִים לַעֲשׂוֹת בָּהֶם כִּרְצוֹנוֹ וְצִוָּנוּ לְהָנִיחַ עַל הַיָּד לְזִכָּרוֹן זְרוֹעַ הַנְּטוּיָה, וְשֶׁהִיא נֶגֶד הַלֵּב לְשַׁעְבֵּד בָּזֶה תַּאֲווֹת וּמַחְשְׁבוֹת לִבֵּנוּ לַעֲבוֹדָתוֹ יִתְבָּרַךְ שְׁמוֹ, וְעַל הָרֹאשׁ נֶגֶד הַמֹּחַ, שֶׁהַנְּשָׁמָה שֶׁבְּמֹחִי עִם שְׁאָר חוּשַׁי וְכֹחוֹתַי כֻּלָּם יִהְיוּ מְשֻׁעְבָּדִים לַעֲבוֹדָתוֹ יִתְבָּרַךְ שְׁמוֹ.

---

16   Originally printed in siddurs that follow the custom of the Ari, such as *Sha'arei Tziyon* and *Likutei Tzvi*. Subsequently it was printed in almost all siddurs. The version here is the one generally recited by Ashkenazim. The Sefardi version appears in Sefardic siddurs.
17   See *Shulchan A'rukh* 25:5.

and below to do with as He pleases. He has commanded us to put tefillin on the arm to remember the out-stretched arm [in Egypt], and that it be near the heart to place all the de-sires and thoughts of our heart at His service, May His Name be blessed; and on the head near the brain, so that the soul that is in my brain, together with my other senses and strengths, be placed at His service, May His Name be blessed.

C. The First Prayer:

May some of the heavenly outpour-ing from the commandment of te-fillin reach me so that I have a long life filled with bountiful holiness, with holy thoughts completely unaf-fected by any hint of sin or evil. Nor should the evil inclination seduce us or incite against us, and may it allow us to serve G-d as our heart desires.

D. The Second Prayer

May it be Your will O Lord, our G-d and G-d of our fathers, that it be considered before the Holy One Blessed Be He as if I fulfilled the commandment of putting on tefillin in all its details, implications and in-tentions, together with all 613 com-mandments that are dependent upon it. Amen, forever.

• בקשה א': וּמִשֶּׁפַע מִצְוַת תְּפִלִּין יִתְמַשֵּׁךְ עָלַי לִהְיוֹת לִי חַיִּים אֲרֻכִּים וְשֶׁפַע קֹדֶשׁ וּמַחֲשָׁבוֹת קְדוֹשׁוֹת בְּלִי הִרְהוֹר חֵטְא וְעָוֹן כְּלָל, וְשֶׁלֹּא יְפַתֵּנוּ וְלֹא יִתְגָּרֶה בָּנוּ יֵצֶר הָרָע, וְיַנִּיחֵנוּ לַעֲבֹד אֶת ה' כַּאֲשֶׁר עִם לְבָבֵנוּ.

• בקשה ב': וִיהִי רָצוֹן מִלְּפָנֶיךָ ה' אֱלֹהֵינוּ וֵאלֹהֵי אֲבוֹתֵינוּ, שֶׁתְּהֵא חֲשׁוּבָה מִצְוַת הֲנָחַת תְּפִלִּין לִפְנֵי הַקָּדוֹשׁ בָּרוּךְ הוּא, כְּאִלּוּ קִיַּמְתִּיהָ בְּכָל פְּרָטֶיהָ וְדִקְדוּקֶיהָ וְכַוָּנוֹתֶיהָ וְתַרְיַ"ג מִצְווֹת הַתְּלוּיוֹת בָּהּ, אָמֵן סֶלָה.

Some say no prayer before putting on the tefillin, other than the blessing itself.[18] Nevertheless they think about the intention of the commandment and its reasons as they recite the blessing and put the tefillin on.[19]

The reason for affirming G-d's unity is to arouse feelings of love and fear of G-d through mentioning the unity of G-d.[20] Even just saying the words has its effects in heaven, despite not understanding these hidden mysteries.[21]

When reciting the beginning of the above prayer, it is necessary to pronounce the twice-mentioned letter ה of the four lettered Name as "kay".[22] Others pronounce no part of the Name.[23]

The reason for verbalizing the intention is to awaken the proper intentions, since a commandment is properly fulfilled only through intentions at the time of performance.[24] Needless to say, verbalizing intentions is only a means to truly having intention. Accordingly, reciting the prayer without thought of the proper intention performs the means but does not accomplish the true purpose.[25]

According to one opinion, the part which lists the four portions should be changed to list them according to the order in which they are written in the Torah. In other words, instead of *Shma, Vehayah im shamo'a, Kadesh, Vehayah ki yeviakha*, one should say *Kadesh, Vehayah ki yeviakha, Shma* and *Vehayah im shamo'a.*[26]

18   See *Noda' Beyehudah* I, *Yoreh De'ah* 93.
19   See *Mishnah Brurah* 25:15.
20   *Pele Yoetz, Dibur*, s.v. *Vehachelek.*
21   *Vayaged Mosheh* (Katz) 11; *Toldos Kol Aryeh* 137:13.
22   *Yalkut Yosef, Tefillin* 31.
23   *Toldos Kol Aryeh* 137:13.
24   *Mishnah Brurah* 25:15.
25   *Beis Barukh* I,14:247.
26   *Tshuvos Divrei Yisrael* 1:24.

Chapter Eight

Putting On the Tefillin

There are different customs concerning how the tefillin should be put on. This chapter will present a step-by-step account, including pictures, of how it should be performed.

Putting on the *Tefillin Shel Yad*

After completing the preparations described in the previous chapter, the *tefillin shel yad* are put on according to the following order:

Removing the Tefillin from the Bag

Open the tefillin bag and put your right hand[1] into the left side of the bag to remove the *tefillin shel yad*. (Needless to say, those whose custom it is to place the *tefillin shel yad* on the right side of the bag[2] should put their hand to the right side of the bag.)

Be careful not to reach for the *tefillin shel rosh* first.[3]
Do not remove the tefillin by shaking them out of the bag.[4]

Kiss the *tefillin shel yad* to show how precious the *mitzvah* is to you.[5]

Removing the Tefillin from its Box

Unwind the strap from around the box and straighten it out along its entire length. This prevents the strap from tangling as it is wound around the arm, which could cause you to stop to untangle the strap. Such stopping involves an undesired break between putting on the *tefillin shel yad* and the *tefillin shel rosh*.[6]

Be careful that the strap does not touch the floor.[7]

The following are the steps used for removing the *tefillin shel yad* from its box:

- Loosen the strap where it is wrapped around the box beneath the *ma'avarta* (so that it not interfere with opening the box).

---

1 A left-handed person uses the left hand. See *Leket Hakemach Hechadash*, 27:6.
2 See Chapter Eleven concerning replacing the tefillin into the bag.
3 *Mishnah Brurah* 28:7 and *Biur Halakhah* 25, s.v. *Shelo yifga.*
4 *Mishnah Brurah* 28:9.
5 *Shulchan A'rukh* 28:3 and the *Kaf Hachayim* thereon (18). Also see *Ben Ish Chai, Chayei Sarah.*
6 *Od Yosef Chai, Vayera* 5.
7 *Kitzur Shelah, Tefillin; A'rukh Hashulchan* 40:1.

- Hold the box with the tefillin slightly inverted (so that there be no danger of the tefillin falling out in the next step).

- Pull open the bottom side of the box (rather than the top side of the box which has more resistance when opening. This resistance, which can wear down the corners, is thereby avoided).

- Carefully remove the tefillin from its box.

If the tefillin fall onto the floor without the box, it is customary to fast.[8] If a person is too weak to fast well, or if he studies Torah all day and fasting would reduce his study time, he may either give charity,[9] study Torah an extra two or three hours that day, or accept upon himself a speech fast (in which all non-Torah speech is forbidden)[10] as a penance instead. (No penance is required if only the straps fell on the floor.)[11]

Preparing the Tefillin for Placement

Remove the protective covering from the *tefillin shel yad* (it is replaced after the *tefillin shel rosh* is put on).[12]

Be sure to hold the uncovered *tefillin shel yad* by its walls and not by the corners. Holding it by the corners wears them down, which over time ruins the squareness.

Make sure that the *yod* of the knot touches the walls of the *bayis*.[13]

Preparing the Arm for Placement

Roll up your left sleeve[14] until above the area in which the tefillin are placed, so that the majority of the upper arm is uncovered. This prevents the sleeve from getting in the way of placing the tefillin directly on the flesh.

When several layers of clothing are worn, as on cold days, make sure that the rolled up sleeves do not subsequently push down the tefillin.

8   *Mishnah Brurah* 40:3.
9   *Kaf Hachayim* 28:5.
10 *Beis Barukh* I p. 377.
11 *Kaf Hachayim* 28:5.
12 See *Tshuvos Tiferes Adam* 1 for an overview on this point. Also see the notes to *Beis Barukh* I, pp. 313-314.
13 *Shulchan A'rukh* 27:2. When there is no alternative other than tefillin in which the *yod* does not touch the walls, it may be used. (*Beis Barukh* 14:75).
14 A left-handed person rolls up his right sleeve.

The hands are generally washed after touching the skin between the elbow and the shoulders. Nevertheless, some do not wash their hands when the skin was touched as part of tefillin placement.[15]

Placing the Tefillin on the Arm

Kiss the *tefillin shel yad*[16] and place it on your left arm[17] so that the *ma'avarta* is closest to the shoulder[18] and the *yod* knot to the heart.[19]

Ashkenazim stand when putting on the tefillin,[20] whereas the Sefardim sit[21].

Place the tefillin on the lower part of the bicep.[22] (Leave the tefillin loose at this stage.)

Make sure that the front of the *titura* does not extend over the lower end of the bicep, which is the end of the placement area.[23] This may be checked in one of two ways: (A) Visually, by flexing the bicep and looking where the swell of the bicep begins, or (B) Measuring the distance between the forearm, and the *titura* edge when the arm is bent at a 90 degree angle. The swell of the average bicep begins two fingers away from the bent forearm.**1**

Obviously, before using the measurement method it is necessary to ascertain that the swell of your bicep in fact begins two fingers away from the bent forearm.

Those who wash their hand when touching the upper arm as part of the tefillin placement (see above) should be careful not to actually touch the upper arm while measuring.

Make sure that the top of the *ma'avarta* does not extend past the midpoint of the upper arm, which is the end of the placement area. **2**

If the entire *tefillin shel yad* was properly placed, but the just the lower tip of the *titura* extends past the beginning of the bicep swell, the mitzvah is not fulfilled and the *brachah* is in vain.[24] If only the upper tip

---

15   The issue is discussed at length in *Minchas Yitzchak*, Volume Four, 114 a and b.
16   *Ben Ish Chai, Chayei Sarah* 10. See *Kaf Hachayim* 28:18.
17   *Shulchan A'rukh* 27:1. A left-handed person places it on his right arm.
18   *Shulchan A'rukh* 27:3.
19   *Shulchan A'rukh* 27:2.
20   *Rama* 25:11.
21   *Kaf Hachayim* 27:33. Also see the *Rama* there.
22   *Shulchan A'rukh* 27:1.
23   *Rama* 27:1; *Mishnah Brurah* 27:4; *Biur Halakhah* 27, s.v. *Bevasar*.
24   *Mishnah Brurah* and *Biur Halakhah*, ibid.

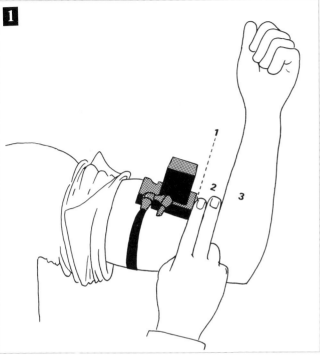

The lowermost point for placing the tefillin on the arm:

The beginning of the bicep swell[1] is the lowermost point for placing the lower part of the tefillin.

It is possible to check if the tefillin goes below the permitted point by checking with two fingers.[2]

Whoever intends to make use of this method, should first make sure that the the distance between the forearm[3] and the lowermost point of the bicep swell is in fact two fingers.

The uppermost point for placing the tefillin on the arm:

The midpoint[1] of the upper arm[2] is the upper limit for placing the upper edge of the tefillin.

Some follow the opinion of the Gra that the upper end of the bicep swell[3] is the uppermost point for placing the tefillin. In difficult situations this opinion may be followed.

of the *ma'avarta* extends too far the mitzvah is only fulfilled *bedia'vad*.[25] Accordingly, it is better to keep the edges of the *titura* and of the *ma'avarta* away from the edges of the placement area. Then, even if the tefillin move somewhat at some point they won't pass the edges of the placement area.[26]

Some tefillin are so large that their length is greater than the distance between the beginning of the bicep swell and the midpoint of the upper arm (this is fairly common in youths with short arms). It is preferable to place the top of such tefillin above the midpoint of the upper arm so that the *titura* does not extend past the beginning of the bicep swell. The former is acceptable *bedia'vad*, whereas the latter is totally unacceptable.[27]

Some follow the Kabbalistic custom of covering the arm with the tallis (assuming, of course, that the individual wears one) while putting the tefillin on the arm and winding the straps, so that the placement should be in private.[28]

Make sure that the *tefillin shel yad* is turned somewhat in the direction of the body.[29] **3**

Keep in mind that when the strap of the tefillin is tightened the tefillin will move somewhat. The direction of movement differs between the Sefardi custom and the Ashkenazi custom of putting on tefillin because of the location of the loop. According to the Sefardi custom the loop is on the side of the arm furthest away from the body and therefore, tightening the loop pulls the tefillin away from the body somewhat. On the other hand, the loop is on the side closest to the body according to Ashkenazi custom. Therefore, tightening the loop pulls the tefillin somewhat closer to the body. Accordingly, one who follows the Sefardi custom should compensate by turning the tefillin slightly more than desired in the direction of the body, whereas one who follows the Ashkenazi custom should compensate by turning the tefillin slightly less than is desired in the direction of the body. In either case, then, tightening the loop will bring the tefillin to the desired spot.

Check that the sleeve did not slip beneath the tefillin or the strap, which would be considered a barrier between the tefillin and skin.[30]

Be certain that the black side of the strap faces outwards along the entire part wrapped around the arm.[31]

---

25 *Mishnah Brurah*, ibid.
26 *Mishnah Brurah* 27:33.
27 *Mishnah Brurah* 27:4.
28 *Kaf Hachayim* 25:32.
29 *Shulchan A'rukh* 27:1. See text accompanying note 43 for instructions about checking this point.
30 See *Shulchan A'rukh* 27:4; *Mishnah Brurah* 27:16.
31 *Shulchan A'rukh* 27:11 and 33:3; *Mishnah Brurah* 27:39.

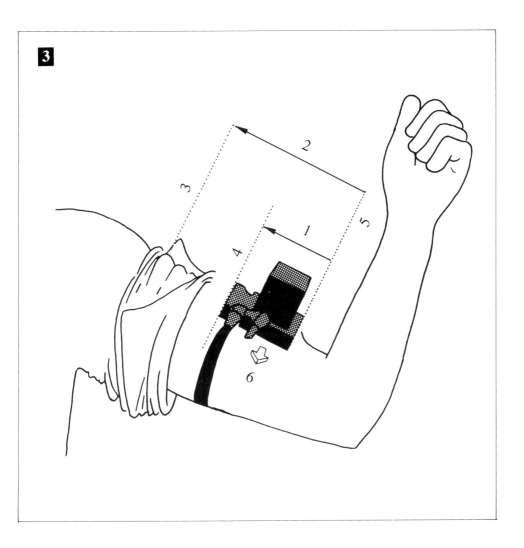

Tefillin Shel Yad Placement: A Summary

1. The place according to the *Shulchan A'rukh* and the *Rama*.
2. The place according to the *Gra*. (Relied upon for difficult circumstances.)
3. The topmost part of the bicep.
4. The midpoint of the upper arm.
5. The lowermost part of the bicep.
6. The tefillin leans towards the body.

The *Brachah*

Hold onto the strap[32] close to the point in which it emerges from the loop ▮4▮ ▮5▮ with the right hand[33] and recite the *brachah*:

ברוך אתה ה אלוקינו מלך העולם אשר קדשנו במצוותיו וצוונו להניחתפלין.[34]

Be careful not to tighten the strap before finishing the *brachah*, because a complete *brachah* must always be recited before performing a *mitzvah*.[35]

Tightening and Winding the Strap

Immediately after reciting the *brachah* the strap is tightened and then wound around the arm as follows:

- Pull at the strap to tighten it around the upper arm.[36]

- Wind the strap seven times for the Ashkenazi custom, and eight times (i.e., seven complete times) for the Sefardi custom.[37] ▮6▮ ▮7▮ ▮8▮ ▮9▮

Wind the strap once or twice, one on top of the other, on the palm, to maintain the tightness of the strap wound around the forearm while putting on the *tefillin shel rosh*.[38] It is the custom of some to insert the strap end beneath the windings around the palm[39]

While tightening the strap, which is the main part of the mitzvah, have in mind to fulfill the mitzvah and think about the reason behind it.[40]

---

32 See *Mishnah Brurah* 206:19 and 167:22.
33 *Mishnah Brurah* 206:18. A left-handed person uses his left hand.
34 *Shulchan A'rukh* 25:5.
35 *Shulchan A'rukh* 25:8.
36 *Shulchan A'rukh* 25:8 and *Mishnah Brurah* 25:25.
37 See *Mishnah Brurah* 27:31 and *Kaf Hachayim* 27:35. The Ashkenazi custom counts the two half windings of the first and last wind as part of the seven, whereas the Sefardi custom does not. Accordingly, they require eight windings so that there be seven complete windings.
38 See *Mishnah Brurah* 25:38.
39 See *Shulchan Hatahor* 25:8 and *Taamei Haminhagim* page 13.
40 *Mishnah Brurah* 25:15. Also see the previous chapter.

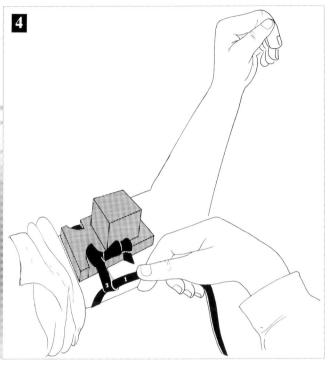

How to Hold the Strap Before the *Brachah*

Ashkenaz Custom

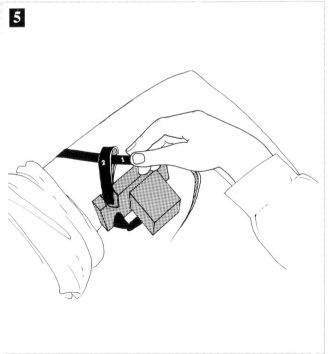

Nusach
Sefard
and Sefardim

Hold the strap[1] near the loop[2]. **According to Ashkenaz custom**: The loop faces the body. **According to *nusach* sefard and sefardim**: The strap faces away from the body.

Although most who pray *nusach* ashkenaz follow the first custom, and most who pray otherwise follow the second custom, there is no clear correspondence.

According to the Ashkenazi custom [the loop is on the body side[א]]: Pull the strap from the loop beneath the arm towards the outside and wind around the arm[1] towards the forearm, then wind seven times[2] towards the body[3]. This is the custom of Ashkenazim, including some who pray *nusach sefard*[ב].

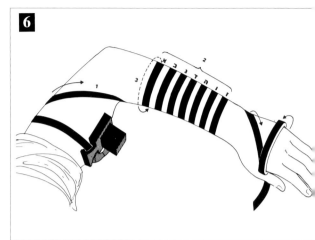

According to the *Sefardi* custom [the loop is on the external side[ג]]: Pull the strap over the arm away from the body[1], wind around the arm[ד] towards the forearm and then wind eight times[ה] (=seven full times)[2] away from the body[3]. This is the custom of most Ashkenazim who pray *nusach sefard*, and most Sefardim[ו].

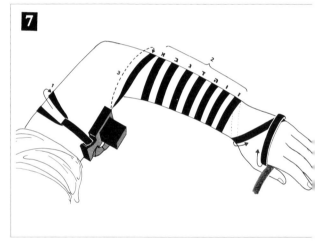

Winding the Tefillin Around the Arm

א. *Darkhei Mosheh*, 27:1; *Biur Halakhah 2*, s.v. *uminhag*. See picture 3.
ב. Such as those that come from Congress Poland.
ג. *Mahari Ben Chaviv*, cited in *Beis Yosef* 27. See also *Sha'arei Teshuvah* 27:8; *Biur Halakhah* 27; *Kaf Hachayim* 27:11; *A'rukh Hashulchan* 27:10.
ד. Some (based on Kaballah)wind the strap three times around the upper arm, in a *shin* shape.
ה. Although it appears as if it is wound eight times, only seven of them are counted. They are called the "seven complete windings" because the half-winding between the upper arm and the forearm as well as the half-winding between the forearm and the palm are not counted.
ו. Such as those from Morocco, Haleb and those areas in which the masses (as opposed to individuals) did not follow Kabbalistic practices.

According to the custom of the *Ben Ish Chai*:[א]

Pull the strap towards the *bayis*[1], wind it over the *bayis* and the *yod* knot[2], continue straight down to the forearm, wind eight times[ב] around the forearm (=seven full times[4]). This is the custom of certain Sefardim who follow *kabbal-lah*[ג].

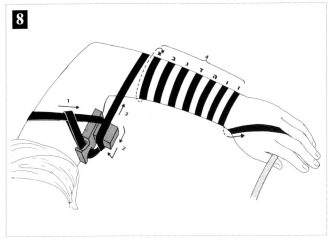

An alternate version:

Pull the strap away from the body[1] wind around the arm to the *bayis*[2], and the *yod*[3]. Wind again around the arm[ד] away from the body,[4] to reach the forearm and wind eight times[ה] around the forearm (=seven full times[5]). This is the custom of Rabbi B.Z. Aba-Shaul and the late Rabbi Y. Zadka[ו].

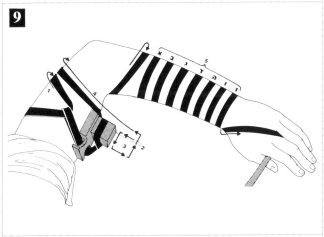

Sefardim Who Follow Kabballah

These are merely the most common customs. There are others.

א. Year 1, *Parashas Vayera*, 15. See *Kaf Hachayim* 25:67 and 27:13.
ב. Although there appear to be eight windings, only seven of them are counted, and hence the name "seven full windings". The half-wind to the forearm and the half-wind to the palm are not counted.
ג. Note ו explains why this custom was not accepted by many of his followers. Nevertheless, Rabbi E. Cohen, a disciple of the *Ben Ish Chai*, placed tefillin on youth in this manner.
ד. Some go straight down to the forearm without additional winding.
ה. See note ב above.
ו. Rabbi B.Z. Aba-Shaul asked the late Rabbi E. Cohen what one who could not properly tighten the *tefillin shel yad* when attempting to follow the custom of the Ben Ish Chai, not to wind on the upper arm, should do. The reply was to follow the example here, so that the tefillin could be properly tightened. (Since he has no alternative, he may wind around the upper arm).

To summarize the essence of the mitzvah and the reason behind it: We are commanded to put on tefillin which contain four *parshiyos* that discuss the unity of G-d and the exodus from Egypt. We put one on the arm near the heart and the other on the head near the brain to demonstrate that we put these two major organs of the body at the service of G-d.[41]

Checking That the *Tefillin Shel Yad* is in the Right Place

After the strap of the *tefillin shel yad* is wound around the arm, one should check that the *tefillin shel yad* is in the right place, as follows:

- Check that the front edge of the *titura* does not pass the front end of the bicep.[42]

- Check that the *tefillin shel yad* turns towards his body[43] by lowering the arm against the body to see if the tefillin touches the body. **10**

Prohibition Against Interruption Between *Yad* and *Rosh* Tefillin

Be careful that there be no break between putting on the *tefillin shel yad* and the *tefillin shel rosh*. This includes winking, hand motions and even quietly doing nothing for no reason.[44] Furthermore, it is even forbidden to respond Amen or any other response as part of the services.[45]

There is no real basis for covering the *tefillin shel yad* before putting on the *tefillin shel rosh*, nevertheless, some do follow such a custom. Those who do, should not pull down their sleeve or put on a jacket (a break); rather they should make a simple minimal motion to push down their sleeve.[46]

41 See *Shulchan A'rukh* 25:5.
42 *Mishnah Brurah* 27:4, and *Biur Halakhah* s.v. *Bevasar*.
43 *Shulchan A'rukh* 27:1.
44 *Shulchan A'rukh* 25:9; *Mishnah Brurah* 25:29.
45 *Shulchan A'rukh* 25:10.
46 *O'ver Orach*, Appendix to *Orchos Chayim Hechadash*, 25; *Yalkut Yosef, Tefillin* 20. Also see *Shea'rim Metzuyanim Bahalakhah, Kuntres Acharon* page 6. An opposing view is defended in *Or Torah Journal*, Elul 5746. Also see the *Kislev* 5746 issue.

Checking That the Tefillin Shel Yad is in the Right Place

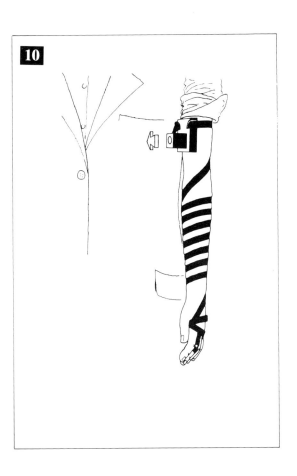

Lower the arm, press it against the body and check whether the tefillin face the body and touch it.

Putting on the *Tefillin Shel Rosh*

The *tefillin shel rosh* is put on immediately after the *tefillin shel yad* as follows:

Removing the *Tefillin Shel Rosh* From the Bag

Take the tefillin shel rosh out of the bag with the right hand[47] and kiss it.[48] Do not remove the tefillin by shaking it out of the bag.[49]

Removing the *Tefillin Shel Rosh* From its Box

Take the straps off of the box.
Be careful that the straps do not drag on the floor.[50]

Open the box and remove the head tefillin as follows:

- Hold the box slightly inverted.

- Open the box from the *titura* side.

- Carefully remove the tefillin from the box.

When holding the tefillin, be careful not to hold the corners, since this could wear them down.

Putting the Tefillin on the Head **11** **12**

Kiss the tefillin shel rosh[51] and while standing,[52] put it above the forehead at the point in which hair grows, directly above a point midway between the eyes.[53]

---

47 A left-handed person removes it with his left hand. See Leket Hakemach Hechadash 27:6.
48 *Shulchan A'rukh* 28:3. See *Kaf Hachayim* 28:18. Kissing is not considered a break, since it is part of the requirements of putting on tefillin. See *Nimukei orach Chaim* 28:2; *Igros Mosheh, Orach Chaim* IV,10.
49 *Mishnah Brurah* 28:9.
50 *Kitzur Shelah, Tefillin; A'rukh Hashulchan* 40:1.
51 *Ben Ish Chai, Chayei Sarah* 10. Also see *Kaf Hachayim* 28:18.
52 Sefardim as well as Ashkenazim. (*Rama* 25:11; *Ben Ish Chai, Chayei Sarah* 9)
53 *Shulchan A'rukh* 27:10. Also see *Siddur* of *Ba'al Hatanya*.

Place for *Tefillin Shel Rosh*

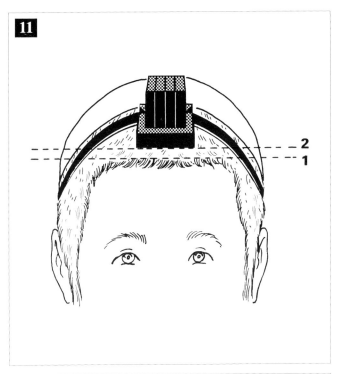

The place length-wise:
The hairline above the fore-head[1] is the front-most part that the front end of the *titura* may be placed.

Preferably, the front end of the *titura* should be placed slightly above the hairline[2] so that if the *tefillin shel rosh* slips downwards somewhat, it will not pass the permitted placement area.

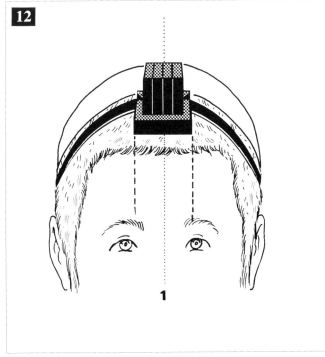

The place width-wise:
The midpoint of the head's width, opposite the area between the eyes, is the tefillin placement area.

When the *tefillin shel rosh* are placed exactly at the midpoint of the head's width, the line that bisects the head width-wise[1] runs through the midpoint of the eyes and through the middle groove between the sections.

The knot on the strap should be placed in back of the head at the bottom part of the skull at its midpoint.[54]   **13**   **14**

Loosely arrange the strap around the head (it will be tightened at a later stage).

A person who lost the hair in front of his head should put the tefillin on the spot where hair used to grow. It is easy to determine that spot, since the skin there is different than the skin of the forehead.[55]

Some have the custom, based upon *Kaballah*, to look at the two *shin*s on the tefillin, first the four-headed one and then the three-headed one, before putting it on.[56]

Some specifically hold the knot in the right hand, and the tefillin in the left hand, when they put it on their head.[57] Others are careful to hold the knot and the tefillin together, put the tefillin on its spot on the head, and only then to move the knot to its proper place.[58]

Another custom based upon *Kaballah* that some have is to place the *Tallis* over the head (those who wear one) when putting the tefillin on the head, so that it can be put on privately.[59]

Make sure that the *yarmulke* did not slip under the tefillin or the strap, so that it not be a barrier between the tefillin and the skin.[60]
Check with your fingers that the black side of the strap surrounding the head faces outwards.[61]

The *Brachah* (According to Ashkenazi Custom)
Touch the straps on either side of the head[62] and quietly[63] recite:
ברוך אתה ה אלוקינו מלך העולם אשר קדשנו במצוותיו וצונו על מצות תפלין.[64]

54   See notes 77 and 78 .
55   *Ben Ish Chai*, op cit. 1; *Os Chaim Veshalom* 27:15.
56   *Kaf Hachayim* 25:35.
57   *Sefer Mitzvas Tefillin Mehashelah*, 8:5.
58   *Kaf Hachayim* 40:1.
59   *Kaf Hachayim* 25:32.
60   *Shulchan A'rukh* 27:4 and *Mishnah Brurah* 27:16.
61   *Shulchan A'rukh* 27:11, and 33:3; *Mishnah Brurah* 27:39.
62   See *Mishnah Brurah* 206:19 and 167:22.
63   *Kitzur Shulchan A'rukh* 10:4.
64   *Rama* 25:5.

Placement of the *Rosh* Knot

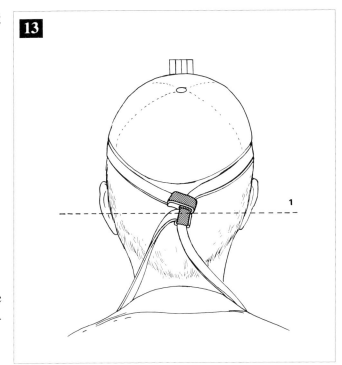

The knot length-wise:
The bottom of the skull[1] above the indentation, is the length-wise place for the knot.

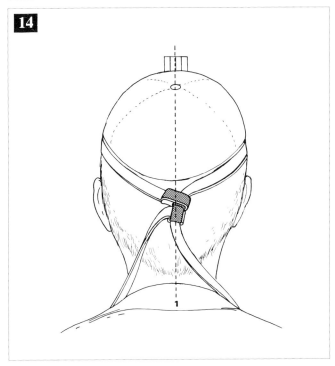

The knot width-wise:
The midpoint of the back of the neck is the correct place for the knot.

When the knot is exactly in place, the line that bisects the back of the head lengthwise passes through the middle of the knot and the middle of the *tefillin shel rosh.*[1]

(No *brachah* is generally recited for the tefillin *shel rosh* according to the Sefardi ritual.[65])

The next to the last word is pronounced *mitzvas* (not *mitzvos*)[66] and the L of tefillin is stressed.[67]

Make sure not to tighten the strap around the head until after reciting the *brachah*.[68]

If the *yarmulke* was removed for putting on the tefillin, make sure to replace it before reciting the *brachah*.[69]

Tightening the Strap

Immediately after reciting the *brachah*, tighten the strap around the head with your fingers, so that neither the tefillin nor the knot will move out of place.[70]

Some tighten the strap with their *yarmulke* covering their fingers to avoid any question of having to wash their hands.[71]

While tightening the tefillin, which is the main requirement, have in mind to fulfill the obligation and also think of the reason for the requirement.[72]

Reciting *Baruch Shem Kevod...* (According to Ashkenazi Custom)

After tightening the strap Ashkenazim recite the following:

ברוך שם כבוד מלכותו לעולם ועד.[73]

---

65 *Shulchan A'rukh* 25:5. Certain Ashkenazim follow this custom as well.
66 *Mishnah Brurah* 25:20.
67 *Mishnah Brurah* 25:19.
68 *Rama* 25:18.
69 *Mishnah Brurah* 25:27.
70 *Mishnah Brurah* 27:35.
71 *Tzitz Eliezer* XII, 6:1 reviews the Halakhic literature on the subject. He explains that although some require washing the hands for any touching of the hair, the majority position is that washing the hands is only required when the head is scratched. (Still others consider tightening the strap equivalent to scratching.)
72 *Mishnah Brurah* 25:15.
73 *Rama* 25:5.

Sefardim, who do not recite a separate *brachah* over the *tefillin shel rosh*, do not recite *Baruch shem...*

Be sure not to recite *Baruch shem kevod malchuso leo'lam va'ed* until after fully tightening the strap.[74]

---

74   *Mishnah Brurah* 25:21.

Determinining Whether the Tefillin *Shel Rosh* is in Place

The following are the methods for checking the placement of the head tefillin:

- Check if the head tefillin is in the midpoint of the hairline, directly above the midpoint between the eyes.[75] This can be done two ways:

  (A) Hold the two sides of the *titura* between the thumb and forefinger, lower those fingers in a straight line down the forehead until the eyebrow level and feel if the tefillin was in fact between the eyes. **15**

  (B) Hold the tefillin between the forefinger and the pinkie and lower the two fingers between them to feel if the tefillin is between the eyes.[76]

- Check with your fingertips if the front end of the *titura* is above the forehead, slightly above the beginning of the hairline.[77] **16**

- Check that most of the knot is above the bottom of the back of the skull,[78] i.e., above the small indentation in the back of the head underneath the skullbone, by pressing the center of the knot with a finger and feeling the pressure against the skullbone. **17**

- Check if the knot is in the midpoint of the back of the head by pressing the bottom of the knot. If you feel it touching the upper part of the indentation,[79] it is centered, because the indentation is at the midpoint of the back of the head.

Arranging the Straps Emerging from the Knot

Arrange the straps that emerge from the knot so that they hang in front,[80] the right strap on the right side, and the left strap on the left side,[81] with their black side facing out.[82]

---

75 See *Shulchan A'rukh* 27:10.
76 It is unnecessary to check in a mirror. See *Divrei Chaim* II, 6; *Divrei Yoel, Orach Chaim*, 4; *Tzitz Eliezer*, XII, 6:2; *Beis Barukh* I, page 325 in the notes. Some nevertheless do.
77 *Shulchan A'rukh* 25:9; *Mishnah Brurah* 25:33. If even the tip of the titura is on the forehead, the requirement for Tefillin was not fulfilled.
78 See *Shulchan A'rukh* 27:10; *Eshel Avraham* (Buchach) 27:10. "Most of the knot" is the implication of *Mishnah Brurah* 27:35; *Kaf Hachayim* 27:42,43; *Az Nidberu* II, 56 and III, 44. Practically, if all of the knot was above the indentation the tefillin would not be snug on the head.
79 See the above footnote. Needless to say, he who insists on all the knot being above the indentation could not check this way. He could check by drawing his finger down in a straight line from the knot to that indentation. See note 54.
80 *Shulchan A'rukh* 27:11.
81 *I'tur.*
82 *Mishnah Brurah* 27:38.

Checking Placement of the Tefillin and of the Knot

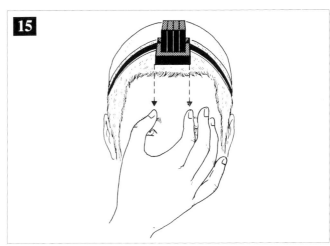

Checking the *tefillin shel rosh* widthwise:

Grasp the sides of the *titura* between two fingers and lower them straight down the forehead to the eyebrows to feel if the same relative area is touched by both fingers.

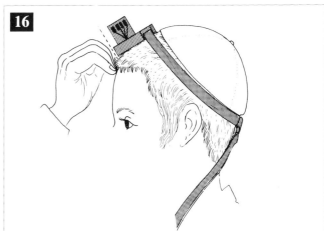

Checking the *tefillin shel rosh* lengthwise:

Touch the hairline and make sure that you are not touching the front end of the *titura*.

Checking the knot in back of the neck:

Press your finger on the center of the knot and check if you feel pressure against the hard bone at the bottom of the skull.

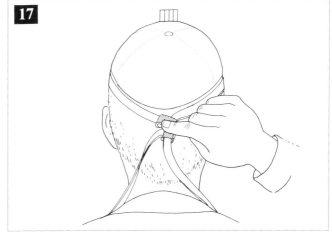

The checking methods illustrated in these pictures are only examples. Each person may check as he sees fit.

Wrapping the Strap Around the Hand

After putting on the *tefillin shel rosh*, unwrap the strap from around the palm and rewrap it, starting with the middle finger,[83] as follows:

Wrapping Around the Finger

Bring the strap from the wrist to the middle finger.[84] ⬛**18** ⬛**19** ⬛**20**
While standing[85] wrap the strap three times around the middle finger. Wind it once around the middle section of the finger (between the first two joints), then wind twice more around its lower section (the part closest to the palm);[86] the first of these two should be near the upper knuckle of this section, and the second should be near the lower knuckle.[87] ⬛**18** ⬛**19** ⬛**20**

This is the most widespread custom, but there are two other customs as well:
(A) First wind twice around the lower section, and then once around the middle section.[88]
(B) First wind once around the lower section, then wind around the middle section, and finally, wind the third time again around the lower joint.[89]

While winding the first loop it is customary to recite: וארשתיך לי לעולם. While winding the second loop recite: וארשתיך לי בצדק ובמשפט ובחסד וברחמים. During the third winding recite: וארשתיך לי באמונה, וידעת את ה'.[90]

Wrapping Around the Palm

After winding the strap around the middle finger, bring it to the palm,[91] wind the remainder of the strap around the palm, leaving a small amount that can be slipped into the straps previously wound around the palm to make sure that the strap and the *tefillin shel yad* remain snugly on the arm.[92] ⬛**18** ⬛**19** ⬛**20**

---

83 *Mishnah Brurah* 27:30; *Kaf Hachayim* 25:68.
84 There are several customs.
85 Sefardim as well as Ashkenazim. (*Elyah Rabah* 27:8; *Kaf Hachayim* 27.)
86 *Mishnah Brurah* 27:30; *Kaf Hachayim* 25:70.
87 *Siddur Derekh Hachayim* and *Siddur Beis Ya'akov*.
88 *Mishnah Brurah, op cit.*
89 *Sefer Mitzvas Tefillin*, p.121, notes.
90 See *Kaf Hachayim* 25:68.
91 Three of the customs for bringing it to the palm are illustrated here.
92 See *Siddur Harav, Hilchos Tefillin; Ketzos Hashulchan* I, *Dinei Tefillin* 12; *Shulchan Hatahor* 27:5 .

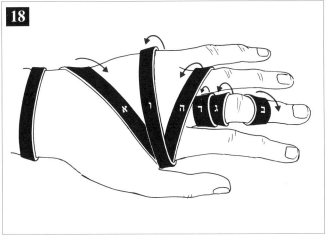

Nusach **Winding Around**
Ashkenaz **the Finger and Hand**

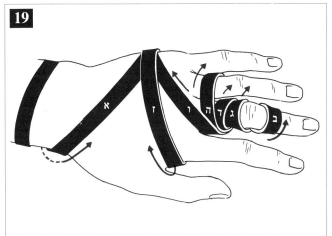

Nusach
Sefard

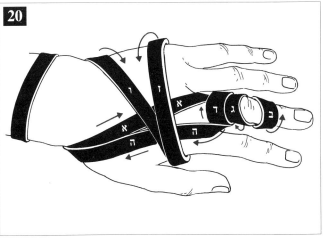

Sefardi

These are the most common customs. There are others.

After Putting on the Tefillin

Between putting on the tefillin and beginning the *Shacharis* service, the following should be done:

- Replace the protective covering of the *tefillin shel yad* to protect its corners from wearing down as a result of friction from the sleeve.

- If possible, put your arm back into the sleeve of your jacket, since it is neither proper to pray with a bare arm,[93] nor with a jacket sleeve hanging down.[94]

- If you wear a tallis, cover your head in one of these three ways:
  (A) Cover your head but not the tefillin, so that the two *shins* remain visible.[95]
  (B) Cover your head and the tefillin, leaving only the front part of the head tefillin visible.[96]
  (C) Cover your head and the tefillin completely, even in front.[97]

Some are careful to wash their hands after putting on tefillin just in case they touched covered parts of the body that require washing the hands.[98]

93 See *A'rukh Hashulchan* 91:6; *Ben Ish Chai, Yisro* 15; *Yaskil A'vdi* VII, p. 329A, and VIII, *Orach Chaim* 24:3. Also see *Yechaveh Da'as* IV, 8.
94 *Kaf Hachayim* 91:26.
95 *Levush* 27:11.
96 *Magen Avraham* 8:3 and the *Machtzis Hashekel* thereon; *Mishnah Brurah* 8:4.
97 The custom of the *Ari*, cited in the *Mishnah Brurah op cit.; Ben Ish Chai, Vayera* 18. The source for this custom is Kaballah.
98 *Os Chayim Veshalom 27:14; Sefer Mitzvas Tefillin*, p. 155 says that that was the custom of the *Chazon Ish*.

Chapter Nine

While Wearing Tefillin

A Jew wearing tefillin is said to be "girded in strength" and "crowned in glory." Furthermore, the sanctity of the tefillin demand that the wearer conduct himself with proper decorum. There are various ways that the wearer can remind himself that he is wearing tefillin, and various requirements for what may and may not be done while wearing tefillin.

Shacharis Service in Tefillin

It is customary to to touch the tefillin with the fingers of the right hand[1] while reciting specific parts of the *Shacharis* service, and then to kiss those fingers after completing the verse. Ashkenazi and Sefardi custom differ as to which places to do this.

According to Ashkenazi custom the following are the places in which the tefillin are touched:

- In the morning blessings, before reciting the blessing that refers to "crowning Yisrael in glory," עוטר ישראל בתפארה, touch the *tefillin shel yad*, while reciting that blessing touch the *tefillin shel rosh*,[2] and then kiss[3] the fingers that touched the tefillin.

- In הודו and in יהי כבוד while reciting the words ישמחו השמים touch the *tefillin shel yad*, and for the words ותגל הארץ touch the tefillin *shel rosh* and kiss the fingers.[4]

- In אשרי, while reciting the words פותח את ידיך, touch the *tefillin shel yad*,[5] and for the words ומשביע לכל חי רצון, touch the *tefillin shel rosh* and kiss the fingers.

- In the first blessing before *Shma*, while reciting יוצר אור, touch the *tefillin shel yad*, and while reciting ובורא חשך, touch the *tefillin shel rosh* and kiss the fingers.[6]

- While saying the words וקשרתם לאות על ידיך, in the first portion of the *Shma*, touch the *tefillin shel yad*, and touch the *tefillin shel rosh*[7] while saying the words והיו לטוטפות בין עיניך, then kiss the fingers.

- While saying the words וקשרתם אותם לאות על ידכם, in the second portion of *Shma*, touch the *tefillin shel yad*, and touch the *tefillin shel rosh*[8] while saying והיו לטוטפות בין עיניכם, then kiss the fingers.

---

1 A left-handed person uses his left hand.
2 Some touch the *tefillin shel yad* while saying the previous blessing, which refers to "being girded in strength," אוזר ישראל בגבורה, then kiss the fingers, and then continue as above. I did not find any source for this. See *Taz* 46:2; *Os Chayim* 25:5.
3 *Chayei Adam* 14:15.
4 See *Likutei Mahariach* I, 50B.
5 *Ta'amei Haminhagim* p. 548.
6 *Baer Hetev* 59:1.
7 *Shulchan A'rukh* 28:1, and 61:25.
8 *Mishnah Brurah* 61:39.

- In the second אשרי of *Shacharis*, while reciting the words פותח את ידיך, touch the *tefillin shel yad*, and for the words ומשביע לכל חי רצון, touch the *tefillin shel rosh* and kiss the fingers.

An alternate custom is to kiss the fingers after touching each tefillin; i.e., kissing after touching the *tefillin shel yad* as well as kissing after touching the *tefillin shel rosh*.[9]

The above places are all the places mentioned in various Ashkenazi sources. Some touch the tefillin in all these places, others touch the tefillin only in some of them. Each individual should follow the custom of his family.

According to Sefardi custom, the tefillin are not touched at all until the blessings recited before *Shma*. They are touched in the following places (in order):

- While reciting יוצר אור, touch the *tefillin shel yad* only, and kiss the fingers.[10]

- Soon afterwards, while reciting קדוש קדוש, touch only the *tefillin shel yad* and kiss the fingers.[11]

- In the same places described for the Ashkenaz custom in the first two portions of *Shma*.

- While saying גאל ישראל, immediately before reciting the *A'midah* prayer touch only the *tefillin shel rosh* and kiss the fingers.[12]

It is customary for some to recite the two portions (of the four inside the tefillin) *Kadesh* and *Vehayah ki yeviacha* immediately after putting the tefillin on. (Others do not recite these portions[13]). Those who do recite these verses, touch the tefillin and kiss their fingers whenever tefillin are mentioned in the verses.[14]

Check that the tefillin are in their right place and tight enough, by touching them periodically throughout the service.[15] Fix them if they moved out of place, but a new blessing is not required.[16]

There is a widespread custom among the Sefardim to take a piece of paper that is larger than the pages of the *siddur* and write either "tefillin" or "intention for tefillin" on it. This paper is placed into the siddur in such a way that the words are visible above the pages of the siddur. As a result, the person remembers the tefillin each time he sees the paper, and can think about their sanctity.[17]

---

9 *Kitzur Shulchan A'rukh* 10:17.
10 *Ben Ish Chai, Shmos*, 1.
11 *Ben Ish Chai, Shmos*, 2.
12 *Ben Ish Chai, Beshalach*, 1.
13 *Kaf Hachayim* 25:30. See *Mishnah Brurah* 25:16.
14 *Likutei Mahariach, Seder Mitzvas Tefillin*, at the end.
15 See *Darkei Chaim Veshalom*, 67.
16 *Mishnah Brurah*, 25:44.
17 *Kaf Hachayim* 28:2.

Decorum While Wearing Tefillin

You must behave in a manner befitting the sanctity of tefillin during the entire time they are on your arm and head, as follows:

- Do not speak idle talk.[18] (It is preferable to say whatever must be said as curtly as possible, and in Hebrew if possible.[19] Some hold onto their tefillin when they must speak, while others speak no secular matters while wearing tefillin.[20])
- Do not behave in a joking, light-headed fashion.[21]
- Do not think inappropriate thoughts.[22]
- Do not fall asleep.[23]
- Do not vent wind.[24]
- Do not eat a meal.[25]

It is not necessary to remove the tefillin for a snack.[26] Nevertheless, some authorities question whether this permission only applies to a time when the tefillin were worn the entire day, but does not apply to people who wear the tefillin only for *Shacharis* services.[27]

If you feel a sudden need to vent wind while wearing tefillin, move the *tefillin shel rosh* to the side and loosen the strap.[28]

It is customary for the one who lifts up the Torah scroll after it is read, and the one who rolls it up, to first remove the strap from their hand, wrap it around their wrist and then slip the end into the wrapped-up part of the strap.[29]

Be careful when standing near a wall in tefillin not to bump against the wall when swaying or bowing. This can mar the corners of the tefillin which could question their acceptability.

---

18 *Mishnah Brurah* 37:7.
19 *Darkei Chaim Veshalom*, 31.
20 *Leket Hakemach Hechadash* 28:1. See also the *Beis Barukh* I, p. 342 in a note.
21 *Mishnah Brurah* 44:3.
22 See *Shulchan A'rukh* 38:4.
23 See *Shulchan A'rukh* 24:4 and the commentaries thereon.
24 *Shulchan A'rukh* 38:2.
25 *Shulchan A'rukh* 40:8.
26 *Shulchan A'rukh* ibid. *Mekor Chayim* thereon writes: "Those who refrain from eating cake or drinking whiskey before removing their tefillin are unnecessarily strict, and are foolish." Also see *Beis Barukh* I, 14:215.
27 *Shulchan Shlomo*, cited in *Mishnah Brurah* 40:19.
28 If possible do the same with the *tefillin shel yad*. See *Minchat Yitzchak*, VI, 13.
29 *Zer Hatorah*, 2. Also heard from Rabbi Chaim Kanievsky citing his father Rabbi Yisrael Yaakov Kanievsky, author of the *Kehillos Yaakov*. Also see *Maharil*, (*Minhagim*) at the end of *Hilchos Lulav*.

Chapter Ten

Removing the Tefillin

Owing to our inability to remain in tefillin for too long a period, it is customary to remain in the tefillin at least until the end of the Shacharis service. The actual removal is the reverse of putting them on: First unwind the strap around the hand, then remove the tefillin shel rosh, *and finally, take off the* tefillin shel yad.

Removing the Tefillin on a Regular Day

It is customary to remain wearing tefillin, if possible, until after reciting the *A'leinu* prayer at the end of *Shacharis*.[1] When the Mourner's *Kaddish* is recited after *A'leinu*, it is preferable to wait until after the *Kaddish*.[2]

Some remain wrapped in tefillin still longer so that they can learn some Torah wearing their tefillin, even if only for a short while.[3]

The Leader (*chazzan*), should not remove his tefillin while standing before the prayer stand.[4]

A person with stomach problems who is afraid that he will not be able to refrain from venting wind may remove his tefillin either after the *A'midah*, after reciting *Ashrei* and *Uva letzion*, or after the completion of the *Kaddish* that follows that. The specific choice is dependent upon the seriousness of his condition.[5]

---

1 *Mishnah Brurah* 25:55; *Kaf Hachayim* 25:88 and 28:9. The reason cited by *Tshuvos Divrei Yisrael* II, p.53 is that the sanctity of *A'leinu* is such (it is the focal point of Rosh Hashanah services) that it should be recited wearing tefillin.
2 *Mishnah Brurah* 25:56.
3 *Kitzur Shelah, Hilchos Tefillin; Mishnah Brurah* 37:7; *A'rukh Hashulchan* 37:3; *Kaf Hachayim* 25:89.
4 *Bikkurei Ya'akov*, 651:29.
5 *Kaf Hachayim* 25:87.

Removing Tefillin on Special Days

On *Rosh Chodesh* (the beginning of the new month) the tefillin are removed after the half *Kaddish* that precedes the Additional *A'midah* (*mussaf*).[6]
When there will be a circumcision immediately after services, it is preferable for all the congregation to remain in their tefillin until after the circumcision.[7]
This custom is based upon the fact that both tefillin (*Shmos* 13:9) and circumcision (*Breishis* 17:11) are referred to as an *os* (sign).

If it is necessary to remove the tefillin before the Torah scroll is returned to the ark on a day in which it is read, do not uncover your head in the presence of the Torah. Rather, the *tefillin shel rosh* should be removed after moving away, or by removal underneath a *tallis*.[8]

There is a dispute concerning removing the tefillin before a covered Torah scroll.[9]

The *tefillin shel yad* may be removed in the presence of a Torah scroll.[10]

---

6 *Mishnah Brurah* 25:59; *Kaf Hachayim* 25:94.
7 *Kaf Hachayim* 25:92; *Beis Barukh* I, p. 388.
8 *Mishnah Brurah* 25:58.
9 *Meishiv Halakhah* I, 386 (referring to a cloth covering) prohibits; *Od Yosef Chai, Chayei Sarah* 2 (referring to enclosure in a box) permits.
10 *Mishnah Brurah* 25:58.

How to Remove the Tefillin

At the end of the *Shacharis* service the tefillin are removed in the following order:

Removing the Strap From the Fingers

The strap around the fingers is the first to be removed. It is removed standing.[11] Some also remove two or three windings of the strap from the forearm.[12] Most Sefardim do this standing as well,[13] whereas others do this seated.[14]

Removing the *Tefillin Shel Rosh*

After removing the straps from the fingers, remove the *tefillin shel rosh*[15] with the left hand, to symbolize the personal difficulty involved in removal.[16] Then kiss the tefillin to symbolize your love for them.[17] One should stand during removal.[18]

Some specifically hold the knot in their right hand while removing the tefillin with their left hand to prevent the knot from hanging down and appearing as if it is being dragged.[19]

Others are careful not to touch the *tefillin shel rosh* at all. Instead, they remove the *tefillin shel rosh* by pulling up the straps that hang in front of them.[20]

Do not remove the *tefillin shel yad* until the *tefillin shel rosh* is removed[21] and placed into the bag.[22]

---

11   Both for Ashkenazim (*Mishnah Brurah* 28:5,6) and for Sefardim (*Kaf Hachayim* 28:5,6).
12   *Kaf Hachayim* 28:6; *Kitzur Shulchan A'rukh* 10:20. But see the *Misgeret Hashulchan* 15, who disputes this.
13   *Kaf Hachayim* 2:6.
14   *Ben Ish Chai, Chayei Sarah* 9.
15   *Mishnah Brurah* 28:5; *Kaf Hachayim* 28:5.
16   *Mishnah Brurah* 28:6; *Kaf Hachayim* 28:8. They also write that a fully left-handed person should remove the *tefillin shel rosh* with the right hand.
17   *Ben Ish Chai, Chayei Sarah* 10. See *Kaf Hachayim* 28:18.
18   Both Ashkenazim and Sefardim (*Shulchan A'rukh* 28:2).
19   *Sefer Mitzvas Tefillin Mehashelah*, 8:5.
20   *Mekor Chayim* 28:2.
21   *Shulchan A'rukh* 28:2.
22   *Mishnah Brurah* 28:8.

Some say that the *tefillin shel rosh* should not be put down until after its straps are wrapped around it and it is placed into the bag.[23] This even applies on *Rosh Chodesh* (the new month) when hurrying to finish removing the tefillin before the congregation begins the *Mussaf* service.[24]

Be careful to hold the tefillin only by the sides and not by the corners. Otherwise, the corners can wear down and negatively affect the acceptability of the tefillin.

Do not let the straps touch the floor.[25]

It is preferable not to speak between removing the *tefillin shel rosh* and *tefillin shel yad*.[26]

Replacing the Tefillin in its Box

The *tefillin shel rosh* is placed into its box as follows:

- Open the empty box and invert it slightly.

- Insert the *bayis* cube into the upper part of the box. (Do not insert the *titura* part first, because that makes it more difficult to close the box, which can wear away the corners.)

- Close the lower part of the box onto the *titura*.

Be careful not to insert the *tefillin shel rosh* into the box of the *tefillin shel yad*.[27]

If as a result of perspiration the *titura* is wet, dry it off first.[28] If possible, it should be left out until it dries.

If it is not dry when placed into the box, the *titura* can warp.

Winding the Straps

Place the knot against the box beneath the *titura*, raise the excess strap from each side of the knot and place it on its respective side of the *titura*. The strap remnants are wrapped around the *titura* on each side.[29]

---

23 *Pri Megadim, Eshel Avraham* 28:4.
24 See the footnotes to *Sefer Mitzvas Tefillin*, at the beginning of page 203.
25 *Kitzur Shelah, Hilkhos Tefillin; A'rukh Hashulchan* 40:1.
26 *Eshel Avraham* (Buchach), 28:2.
27 See *Mishnah Brurah* 42:2.
28 See *Mekor Chaim*, end of 39 in the *Kitzur Halakhos*.
29 *Kitzur Shelah, Hilchos Tefillin*. Also see *Mekor Chaim* 28:2; *Mishnah Brurah* 28:9; *Kaf Hachayim* 28:10.

Some specifically put the knot on top of the *ma'avarta*, rather than beneath it, since they consider it improper to put the knot, with its form of a *dalet* from the four-lettered name of G-d (see Chapter Four), beneath the *ma'avarta*.[30]

Some wind the straps and leave it off the *ma'avarta* so that they resemble the wings of a dove.[31]

Be careful not to wind the straps on the tefillin itself, since the sanctity of the tefillin itself is greater than the sanctity of the straps.[32]

Make sure not to hold the strap and turn the tefillin into it. Instead hold the tefillin and wind the strap around it,[33] because it is better that the strap should be turned and not the tefillin itself.[34]

Do not stretch the straps too much when winding them, as this can stretch the strap and shrink the width to less than the minimal acceptable width for fulfilling the requirement. (According to the Chazon Ish that is 11 millimeters, whereas according to Rabbi Chaim Naeh it is 10—or at the very least 9—millimeters.)

Make sure to place the tefillin into the bag immediately after taking it off and winding it. Do not leave it lying around for later attention. If it is nevertheless impossible to wind the tefillin immediately after removing it, it should still be placed into the bag and not left in the open.[35] Similarly, make sure that the straps do not hang down from the table.[36] (It is not necessary to make sure that the straps of the *tefillin shel yad* not lay on the straps of the *tefillin shel rosh*.[37])

One should wind the tefillin and place it into the bag himself, rather than give it to someone else to do. This indicates greater love for the requirement.[38]

Placing the Tefillin into the Bag

Kiss the *tefillin shel rosh*[39] and place it into the right side of the bag,[40] so that the *ma'avarta* side faces the opening of the bag.[41] The custom of some is to place the *tefillin shel rosh* on the left side of the bag.[42]

---

30 *A'rukh Hashulchan* 28:8.
31 *Mishnah Brurah* 28:9; *A'rukh Hashulchan* 28:8. See *Os Chayim* 28:1 who maintains that the wound straps resemble wings even when wrapped on the *ma'avarta*.
32 *Mishnah Brurah* 28:9; *Kaf Hachayim* 28:10.
33 *Mishnah Brurah* 28:9.
34 *Shulchan A'rukh Harav* 28:7.
35 *Leket Hakemach Hechadash* 28:14.
36 *Od Yosef Chai, Chayei Sarah* 12.
37 *Da'as Kedoshim* 28:2.
38 *Divrei Chaim* cited in *Nimukei Orach Chaim* 28:1; *Ben Ish Chai, Chayei Sarah* 19.
39 *Shulchan A'rukh* 28:3. See *Kaf Hachayim* 28:18.
40 *A'rukh Hashulchan* 25:19 and 28:8; *Os Chayim Veshalom* 28:3.
41 *Leket Hakemach Hechadash* 28:10.
42 *Shulchan Shlomo*, cited in *Mishnah Brurah* 28:7; *Siddur Beis Oved, Hilchos Tefillin*.

Make sure to be consistent about the side to place the *tefillin shel rosh*, and do not change it from side to side. Otherwise, it is conceivable that you will confuse which is which and remove the *tefillin shel rosh* from the bag first, instead of the *tefillin shel yad*.[43]

When the bag is too far away, make sure to get it with the free hand, not the hand holding the tefillin.[44]

Removing the *Tefillin Shel Yad*

After replacing the *tefillin shel rosh* into the bag, the *tefillin shel yad* is removed[45] as follows:

Removing the Tefillin From the Hand

Remove the *tefillin shel yad* and kiss it.[46] Ashkenazim stand while removing the *tefillin shel yad*,[47] whereas Sefardim sit.[48]

Do not remove the tefillin by shaking the arm so that the tefillin falls off and is caught by the other hand.

Be careful that the strap does not touch the floor.[49]

Make sure that the *yod* of the knot is flush against the walls of the tefillin, since some require that the *yod* never move away from the walls of the tefillin, not even when it is in the bag.[50]

The *yod* is more likely to move away from the walls of the tefillin for those who follow the Ashkenaz custom than for those who follow the Sefard custom. When tefillin are put on according to Ashkenaz custom, pulling the strap to tighten it pulls the knot away from the tefillin. On the other hand, since the loop is on the other side from the knot in Sefard tefillin, pulling the strap tightens the knot and pulls the *yod* closer to the wall of the *bayis*.[51]

43   *Kaf Hachayim* 28:18.
44   *Od Yosef Chai, Chayei Sarah*, 5.
45   *Mishnah Brurah* 28:8.
46   *Ben Ish Chai, Chayei Sarah*, 10; See *Kaf Hachayim* 28:18.
47   *Mishnah Brurah* 28:6.
48   *Kaf Hachayim* 28:7
49   *Kitzur Hashelah, Hilchos Tefillin; A'rukh Hashulchan* 40:1.
50   *Mishnah Brurah* 27:10; *Biur Halakhah* 27, s.v. *Haminhag*.
51   *Biur Halakhah*, ibid.

Replacing the Tefillin in its Box

Put the tefillin back into its box as follows:

- Open the empty box and invert it slightly.
- Insert the *bayis* cube into the upper part of the box.
- Close the lower part of the box onto the *titura*.

Winding the Strap

Wind the strap around the *titura* on the side opposite the side of the *yod* knot.[52]

Some do not wind the strap around the *titura*, rather, they wind the strap into a circle of its own and place it beneath the tefillin box.[53]

Placing the Tefillin into the Bag

Kiss the tefillin[54] and put it into the bag next to the *tefillin shel rosh*,[55] so that the *tefillin shel yad* is closer to the opening than the *tefillin shel rosh* is. As a result, when subsequently taking out the tefillin to put them on, you will reach the *tefillin shel yad* first.[56]

---

52 *Divrei Chaim*, cited in the notes to *Sefer Mitzvas Tefillin* p.203.
53 See *Os Chayim Veshalom* 28:1.
54 *Shulchan A'rukh* 28:3; See *Kaf Hachayim* 28:18.
55 *Mishnah Brurah* 28:7.
56 *Shulchan A'rukh* 28:2 and *Mishnah Brurah* thereon.

Glossary

A'midah —See **Shmoneh Esrei**.

Ari — Sixteenth century Rabbinic authority whose script type was adopted by most Chassidim for tefillin.

Ashkenaz — Germany. European Jewry in general is referred to as **Ashkenazi**. Plural – **Ashkenazim**.

Ashuri — The type of script reserved for Torah scrolls, mezuzos and tefillin. See **Stam**.

Bayis — The housing for the **parshiyos**. Plural – **batim**.

Beis Yosef — The major work of the author of the Shulchan A'rukh. The script type described by him was adopted by most of **Ashkenazi** Jewry for tefillin.

Dakos — **Batim** made from several pieces of leather from a small animal, covered with one large piece of leather.

Dalet — One of the three letters of the name of G-d used in conjunction with tefillin. The knot on the tefillin **shel rosh** is either a single or double **dalet** depending on the custom.

Gassos — **Batim** made from one strong thick piece of leather from a large animal (e.g. ox).

Kadesh — One of the four **parshiyos** in the tefillin. It involves the transition from a people in Egypt to an independent nation.

Kesher — The knot on the straps of the tefillin. It forms a **yod** on the tefillin **shel yad** and a **dalet** on the tefillin **shel rosh**.

Ma'avarta — The part of the **bayis** that protrudes from the square **titura** through which the strap passes.

Mikshah — **Batim** whose leather is thick enough not to require an additional piece of leather between the upper and lower **titura**.

Nusach — Version, usually the prayer version of the siddur. **Ashkenazi** Jewry has **Nusach Ashkenaz** and **Nusach Sefard**, whereas the version of **Sefardi** Jewry is generally referred to as **Nusach Edos Hamizrach**.

Parashah — A portion from the Torah. There are four **parshiyos** in each of the two tefillin.

Peshutos — **Batim** made from glued together pieces of leather.

Rabeinu Tam — The grandson of **Rashi**. Tefillin made according to his ruling differed in several ways from those of **Rashi**.

Rashi — A renowned twelfth century scholar and commentator. Standard tefillin are designed in accordance with his ruling.

Retzua'h — Leather strap.

Se'ar E'gel — Calf's hairs that are used to wrap each **parashah**. In the **shel rosh** the ends protrude through the front of the **titura**.

Sefard — Spain. Eastern Jewry and North African Jewry are generally referred to as **Sefardi** or **Sefardic**. Plural – **Sefardim**. Also see **Nusach**.

Stam — An acronym for Sefer Torah (Torah scroll), **Tefillin** and **Mezuzos**, which share various laws. The scribe who writes them is known as a **Sofer Stam**.

Shel Rosh — The tefillin (actually tefillah – singular) worn on the head.

Shel Yad — The tefillin (actually tefillah – singular) worn on the arm.

Shma' — One of the four **parshiyos** of the tefillin. It involves a declaration of the unity of G-d.

Shmoneh Esrei — The eighteen (original plus one later) brachos that are the central portion of the prayers.

Titura — The square part beneath the tefillin cube.

Vehayah I'm Shamo'a — One of the four **parshiyos** of the tefillin. It involves accepting the yoke of the mitzvos.

Vehayah Ki Yeviacha — One of the four **parshiyos** of the tefillin. It involves the Exodus.

Yod — One of the three letters of the name of G-d used in conjunction with tefillin. The knot on the tefillin **shel yad** is in the shape of a **yod** and is known as the **yod** of the **kesher**.